Thérèse de Dillmont's
Encyclopedia of Needlework

Volume I

NEEDLEWORK
&
EMBROIDERY

edited by

MARY GOSTELOW

Alphabooks

This three-volume edition of Thérèse de Dillmont's Encyclopedia of
Needlework © (1982) Alphabooks, Sherborne, Dorset, Britain
comprising Vol 1: Needlework and Embroidery
Vols 2 and 3: Knitting and Crochet and Lacemaking
Introduction and editorial additions © Mary Gostelow 1982

ISBN 0 906670 27 6

Cover illustration: embroidery designed by Mary Gostelow and Tony
Birks-Hay, stitched by Joan Hall in DMC stranded cottons 334 (pale
blue), 352 (geranium), 552 (pale purple), 554 (dark purple), 603 (bright
pink), 726 (yellow), 906 (green) and Blanc (white) on evenweave linen.

Photoset by Photosetting and Secretarial Services, Yeovil, Somerset
Printed and bound in Britain by Butler and Tanner, Ltd., Frome,
Somerset

Contents

Introduction

by Mary Gostelow

Thérèse de Dillmont's 'Encyclopedia', sometimes called simply 'The DMC', has for what seems like time immemorial been *the* standard primer for all types of decorative hand needleworks. I personally was acquainted with Mlle. de Dillmont's book as soon as I learned to stitch.

Since its original publication in 1886, in German, more than a million copies have been sold. Many of these are in a very small, 4 × 3 inch format which renders the text and some of the illustrations more difficult to follow than those in the copy I have in front of me as I write, one of the larger, octavo editions.

Thérèsia Maria Josefa Dillmann von Dillmont* was born in Wiener Neustadt, Austria, in 1846. When she was eleven her father, a Transylvanian nobleman who had exchanged the academic for the military life, died, and Mme von Dillmont took her five young children to Vienna. Thérèse may have attended the Imperial and Royal School of Art Needlework in Vienna: she may even have had a grant from Emperor Franz Josef to help in her ambition to govern and teach. Later she and her sister Francziska, who published as Fanny von Dillmont, opened an embroidery studio.

Sometime before 1884 Thérèse moved to Mulhouse, in Alsace, at that time under German occupation. In that year she entered into an agreement with Dollfus-Mieg et Cie (DMC), a long-established firm which had been manufacturing embroidery threads since 1841. Mlle de Dillmont was to produce a DMC library of specialist as well as general needlework publications. She died in 1890, four months after her marriage to a Viennese businessman, Joseph Friedrich Scheuermann.

*I am indebted to Mrs R. K. Hellmann and The Needle and Bobbin Club for permission to include material which appeared in the club's *Bulletin*, Vol. 59, nos. 1/2, 1976, 21ff.

INTRODUCTION

Of all her publications it is for the Encyclopedia that she is, with justification, best known. It is without doubt a classic. But in any practical art field even a classic needs updating. Having been asked to edit Mlle de Dillmont's work I set myself a rigid brief. Wherever possible I have not attempted to alter the content of her text. Minor grammatical and editorial points which probably arose from translation have been changed in order to make the text flow and for clarification. Only such gross inaccuracies as mislabelled diagrams in the original have been corrected. Although some commodities such as whalebone and spindles for gold work are rarely found today, I have left such references for the sake of tradition and to retain the flavour of the original. I have also left such characteristic usages as the word 'stuff' used throughout in place of our 'fabric' or 'material'.

Mlle de Dillmont suggested with each detailed design suitable stuffs and threads to sew on them. As far as materials are concerned I have taken out specific references as supply varies from country to country, if not from one area to another. Specific suggestions for DMC stranded cottons (floss), the most popular embroidery thread, are inserted where relevant in the main text and captions. Many of Mlle de Dillmont's original colour numbers have been discontinued and I have taken the liberty of indicating substitutes.

One chapter, 'Additional Useful Information', is solely mine. I feel that instructions for waste knots and waste tails and how to mitre corners, for instance, belong in such a classic. By contrast, Mlle de Dillmont's chapters on knitting, crochet, macramé and lace warrant a book of their own and they therefore do not appear here.

Lastly, I feel that every good book, be it concerned with embroidery or whatever, needs a detailed *index*. This is now the *key* to the Encyclopedia. Turn first to it, and I hope you too will find what you want.

Mary Gostelow
Milton Abbas 1982

Preface

The absolute want of any comprehensive book on needlework – such a one as contains both verbal and pictorial descriptions of everything included under the name of needlework – has led me to put into the serviceable form of an Encyclopedia all the knowledge and experience which years of unceasing study and practice have enabled me to accumulate on the subject, with the hope that diligent female workers of all ages may be able by its means to instruct themselves in every branch of plain and fancy needlework.

All the patterns given, even the most insignificant, were worked afresh for the purpose, and thus not merely faithful representations but also lucid and intelligible explanations of the same are secured.

In order that my readers may have something besides the dull theory, the work is enlivened by a number of useful patterns, some new, some derived from the artistic productions of such countries and epochs as have become famous by special excellence in the domain of needlework.

Though, at first sight, the reproduction of many of these patterns may seem to present insuperable difficulties, they will, after a careful study of the text and exact attention to the directions given, prove easy to carry out.

Many of these interesting designs are drawn from private collections whose owners, with great kindness, placed their treasures at my disposal, to copy and borrow from at discretion, for which I desire to take the present opportunity of tendering them my warmest thanks.

The choice of colours and material – a difficult matter to many – my readers will find rendered comparatively easy to them by the notes affixed to the illustrations; and I may point out that most of the patterns were worked with DMC cottons, which enjoy the well-earned reputation of being the very best of their kind in the market of the world.

Experience has convinced me that, in many instances, these cottons may with advantage take the place of wool, linen thread, and even silk.

If this work meet with indulgent judges, and prove really useful, I shall find ample reward in that fact for the trouble and difficulties that have unavoidably attended its completion.

Thérèse de Dillmont

Strip showing running, stitching, button-holing and herring-boning

Plain Sewing

Position of the body and hands. Before describing the different kinds of stitches, a word should be said as to the position of the body and hands when at work. Long experience has convinced me that no kind of needlework necessitates a stooping or cramped attitude. To obviate which, see that your chair and table suit each other in height, and that you so hold your work as hardly to need to bend your head at all. The practice of fastening the work to the knee, besides being ungraceful, is injurious to the health.

Needles. These should be of the best quality. To test a needle, try to break it; if it resist, and then break clean in two, the steel is good; if it bend without breaking, or break without any resistance, it is bad. Never use a bent needle, it makes ugly and irregular stitches, and see that the eye, whether round or egg-shaped, be well-drilled, that it may not fray or cut the thread. The needle should always be a little thicker than the thread, to make an easy passage for it through the stuff. Blackened needles can be made quite bright again by drawing them through an emery cushion.

Scissors. Scissors are a very important accessory of the work-table, and two varieties are indispensable; a pair of large ones for cutting-out, with one point blunt and the other sharp, the latter to be always held downwards; and a pair of smaller ones with two sharp points. The handles should be large and round; if at all tight, they tire and disfigure the hand.

Thimble. Steel thimbles are the best; bone are very liable to break, and silver ones are not deeply enough pitted to hold the needle. A thimble should be light, with a rounded top and flat rim.

10

The thread. Except for tacking, your thread should never be more than from 40 to 50 cm. long. Wool thread has a nap. You can determine this best by running the thread over your upper lip or another sensitive area. Thread the needle so that the thread runs smooth from the needle to the attached (long) end. If the thread is cotton and in skeins, it does not matter which end you begin with, but if you use reeled cotton, thread your needle with the end that points to the reel, when you cut it, as the other end will split and unravel, when twisted from left to right, which is generally done to facilitate the process of threading. The cotton should always be cut, as it is weakened by breaking.

Fig. 1. Knotting the thread into the needle

Knotting the thread into the needle (fig. 1). When the thread becomes inconveniently short, and you do not want to take a fresh one, it may be knotted into the needle thus: bring it round the forefinger close to the needle, cross it on the inside next to the finger, hold the crossed threads fast with the thumb, draw the needle out through the loop thus formed, and tighten the loop round both ends.

Position of the hands (fig. 2). The fabric should be held between the forefinger and the thumb, and left hanging down, over the other fingers. If it need to be more firmly held, draw it between the fourth and fifth fingers, which will prevent it from getting puckered or dragged.

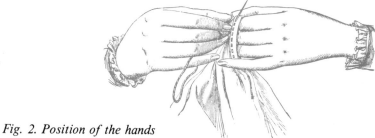

Fig. 2. Position of the hands

Stitches. Plain-sewing comprises 4 varieties of stitches, (1) running, (2) back-stitching, (3) hemming and (4) top or over-sewing.

11

(1) **Running-stitch** (fig. 3). This is the simplest and easiest of all. Pass the needle in and out of the material, at regular intervals, in a horizontal direction, taking up three or four threads at a time. If the stuff allow, several stitches may be taken on the needle at once, before the thread is drawn out. Running-stitch is used for plain seams, for joining light materials, for making gathers and for hems.

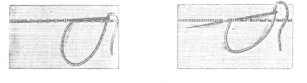

Fig. 3. Running-stitch   Fig. 4. Back-stitch

(2) **Back-stitch** (fig. 4). Insert the needle, and draw it out six threads further on, carry your thread back, from left to right, and insert the needle three threads back from the point at which it was last drawn out, and bring it out six threads beyond.

Stitching (fig. 5). The production of a row of back-stitches that exactly meet one another constitutes what is sometimes called stitching. Only one stitch can be made at a time, and the needle must be put in exactly at the point where it was drawn out to form the preceding back-stitch, and brought out as many threads further on as were covered by the last back-stitch. The beauty of stitching depends on the uniform length of the stitches, and the straightness of the line formed, to ensure which it is necessary to count the threads for each stitch, and to draw a thread to mark the line. If you have to stitch in a slanting line across the stuff, or the stuff be such as to render the drawing of a thread impossible, a coloured tacking thread can be run in first, to serve as a guide.

Stitched hem (fig. 6). Make a double turning, as for a hem, draw a thread two or three threads above the edge of the first turning, and do your stitching through all three layers of stuff; the right side will be that on which you form your stitches.

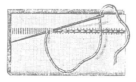 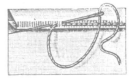

Fig. 5. Stitching   Fig. 6. Stitched hem

(3) **Hemming-stitch** (fig. 7). To make a good hem, your stuff must be cut in the line of the thread. Highly dressed stuffs, such as linen and calico, should be rubbed in the hand to soften them, before the hem is laid. Your first turning should not be more than 2 mm. wide; turn down the whole length of your hem, and then make the second turning of the same width, so that the raw edge is enclosed between two layers of stuff.

Narrow hems do not need to be tacked, but wide ones, where the first turning should only be just wide enough to prevent the edge from fraying, ought always to be. In hemming you insert the needle and thread directed in a slanting position towards you, just below the edge of the hem, and push it out two threads above, and so on to the end, setting the stitches two or three threads apart in a continuous straight line. To ensure the hem being straight, a thread may be drawn to mark the line for the second turning, but it is not a good plan, especially in shirt-making, as the edge of the stuff, too apt in any case to cut and fray is thereby still further weakened. Hems in woollen materials, which will not take a bend, can only be laid and tacked, bit by bit. In making what are called rolled hems, the needle must be slipped in so as only to pierce the first turning, in order that the stitches may not be visible on the outside.

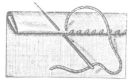

Fig. 7. Hemming-stitch   Fig. 8. Flat seam

Flat seam (fig. 8). Lay your two edges, whether straight or slanting, exactly even, tack them together with stitches 2 cm. long, distant 1 to 2 cm. from the edge, and then back-stitch them by machine or by hand, following the tacking-thread. Cut off half the inner edge, turn the outer one in, as for a hem, and sew it down with hemming-stitches.

Smooth the seam underneath with the forefinger as you go, to make it lie quite flat. Beginners should flatten down the seam with their thimbles, or with the handle of the scissors, before they begin to hem, as the outer and wider edge is very apt to get pushed up and bulge over in the sewing, which hides the stitches.

Rounded seam. Back-stitch your two edges together, as directed above, then cut off the inner edge to a width of four threads, and roll the outer one in, with the left thumb, till the raw edge is quite hidden, hemming as you roll. This kind of seam, on the wrong side, looks like a fine cord, laid on, and is used in making the finer qualities of under-clothing.

Fastening threads off, and on (fig. 9). Knots should be avoided in whitework. To fasten off, in hemming, turn the needle backwards with the point up, take one stitch, and stroke and work the end of the thread in, underneath the turning. To fasten on, in back-stitching or running, make one stitch with the new thread, then take both ends and lay them down together to the left, and work over them, so that they wind in and out of the next few stitches.

   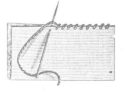

Fig. 9. Fastening threads off and on   *Fig. 10. Top or over-sewing stitch*

(4) **Top or over-sewing stitch** (fig. 10). This stitch is used for joining selvedges together. To keep the two pieces even, it is better either to tack or pin them together first. Insert the needle under the first thread of the selvedge and through both edges, setting your stitches not more than three threads apart. The thread must not be drawn too tightly, so that when the seam is finished and flattened with the thimble, the selvedges may lie side by side.

Another kind of sewing stitch (fig. 11). For dress-seams and patching. Tack or pin the edges together first before sewing, and hold them tightly with the thumb and finger to keep them perfectly even.

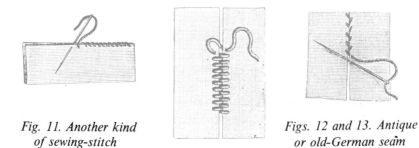

Fig. 11. Another kind   *Figs. 12 and 13. Antique*
of sewing-stitch   *or old-German seam*

Antique or old-German seam (figs. 12 and 13). Tack or pin the selvedges together as above, then, pointing your needle upwards from

14

below, insert it, two threads from the selvedge, first on the wrong side, then on the right, first through one selvedge, then through the other, setting the stitches two threads apart. In this manner, the thread crosses itself between the two selvedges, and a perfectly flat seam is produced. Seams of this kind occur in old embroidered linen articles, where the stuff was too narrow to allow for any other. A similar stitch, fig. 13, only slanting, instead of quite straight as in fig. 12, is used in making sheets.

French double seam (fig. 14). For joining fabrics that fray, use the so-called French seam.

Run your two pieces of stuff together, the wrong sides touching, and the edges perfectly even, then turn them round just at the seam, so that the right sides come together inside, and the two raw edges are enclosed between, and run them together again. See that no threads are visible on the outside. This seam is used chiefly in dress-making, for joining light materials together which cannot be kept from fraying by any other means.

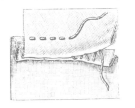

Fig. 14. French double seam

Fig. 15. Hemmed
double seam

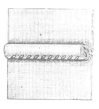

Fig. 16. Open
hemmed double seam

Hemmed double seam (figs. 15 and 16). Turn in the two raw edges, and lay them one upon the other, so that the one next to the forefinger lies slightly higher than the one next to the thumb. Insert the needle, not upwards from below but first into the upper edge, and then, slightly slanting, into the lower one. This seam is used in dress-making for fastening down linings. Fig. 16 shows another kind of double seam where the two edges are laid together, turned in twice, and hemmed in the ordinary manner, with the sole difference that the needle has to pass through a sixfold layer of stuff.

Gathering (fig. 17). Gathers are made with running-stitches of perfectly equal length; take up and leave three or four threads, alternately, and instead of holding the stuff fast with your thumb, push it on to the needle as you go and draw up your thread after every four or five stitches.

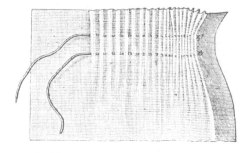

Fig. 17. Gathering

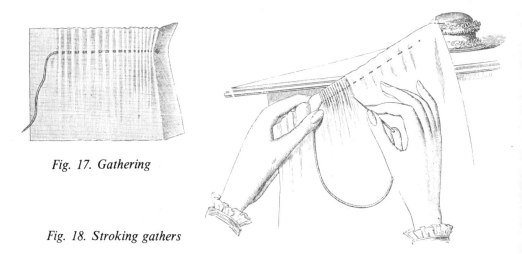

Fig. 18. Stroking gathers

Stroking gathers (fig. 18). When you have run in your gathering thread, draw it up tight, and make it fast round the forefinger of your left hand, and then stroke down the gathers with a strong needle, so that they lie evenly side by side, pushing each gather, in stroking it, under your left thumb, whilst you support the stuff at the back with your other fingers.

Running in a second gathering thread (fig. 19). This is to fix the gathers after they have been stroked, and should be run in 1 or 2 cm. below the first thread, according to the kind of stuff and the purpose it is intended for. Take up five or six gathers at a time, and draw your two threads perfectly even, so that the gathers may be straight to the line of the thread.

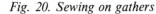

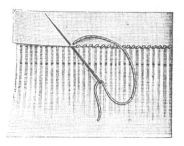

Fig. 19. Running in a second gathering thread   Fig. 20. Sewing on gathers

Sewing on gathers (fig. 20). To distribute the fullness equally, divide the gathered portion of material, and the band or plain piece on to which it is to be sewn, into equal parts, and pin the two together at corresponding distances, the gathered portion under the plain, and hem each gather to the band or plain piece, sloping the needle to make the thread slant, and slipping it through the upper threads only of the gathers.

Whipping (fig. 21). Whipping is another form of gathering, used for fine materials. With the thumb and forefinger of the left hand, roll the edge over towards you into a very tight thin roll, insert the needle on the inside of the roll next the thumb, and bring it out on the outside next the forefinger, at very regular distances, and draw up the thread slightly, from time to time, to form the gathers.

Ornamental hem (fig. 22). For an ornamental hem, make a turning, 2 or 3 cm. deep, and run in a thread, with small running-stitches up and down, as shown in fig. 22. By slightly drawing the thread, the straight edge will be made to look as if it were scalloped.

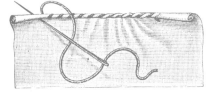

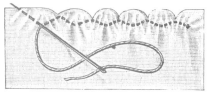

Fig. 21. Whipping   *Fig. 22. Ornamental hem*

Sewing on cord (fig. 23). For sewing on cord, use strong thread. Be careful not to stretch the cord, but to hold it in as you sew it, as it invariably shrinks more than the stuff in the first washing. Fasten it with hemming stitches to the edge of the turning, taking care that it does not get twisted.

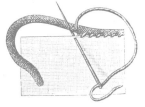

Fig. 23. Sewing on cord

Sewing on flaps (fig. 24). These should be back-stitched on to the right side of the article they are to be affixed to, quite close to the edge, then folded over in half, and hemmed down on the wrong side. Like the cord, the flap must, in the process, be held in very firmly with the left hand. Though the back-stitching could be more quickly done by machine, hand-work is here preferable, as the holding in cannot be done by machine.

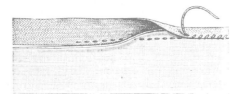

Fig. 24. Sewing on flaps

Sewing on tape-loops (figs. 25 and 26). These, in the case of the coarser articles of household linen, are generally fastened to the corners. Lay the ends of your piece of tape, which should be from 15 to 17 cm. long, side by side, turn in and hem them down on three sides: the loop should be so folded as to form a three-cornered point, as shewn in the illustration. Join the two edges of the tape together in the middle with a few cross-stitches, and stitch the edge of the hem of the article to the loop, on the right side.

Fig. 26 shows how to sew on a loop in the middle of an article.

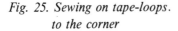
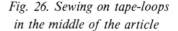

*Fig. 25. Sewing on tape-loops.
to the corner*

*Fig. 26. Sewing on tape-loops
in the middle of the article*

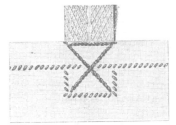

Fig. 27. Strings and loops on fine under-linen

Strings and loops for fine under-linen (fig. 27). Sew these on, likewise, on the wrong side of the article, hemming down the ends, and fastening them on the right side with two rows of stitching crossing each other, and a third row along the edge.

Button-holes in linen (fig. 28). Cut your hole perfectly straight, and of exactly the diameter of the button, having previously marked out the place for it with two rows of running-stitches, two or three threads apart. Put in your needle at the back of the slit, and take up about three threads, bring the working thread round, from right to left, under the point of the needle, and draw the needle out through the loop, so that the little knot comes at the edge of the slit, and so on to the end, working from the lower left-hand corner to the right. Then make a bar of button-hole stitching across each end, the knotted edge towards the slit.

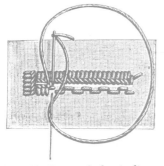 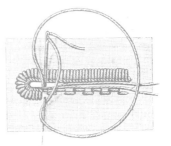

Fig. 28. Button-holes in linen   *Fig. 29. Button-holes in dress materials*

Button-holes in dress materials (fig. 29). Mark out and cut them as described above. If, however, the material be liable to fray, wet the slit as soon as you have cut it with liquid gum, and lay a strand of strong thread along the edge to make your stitches over. One end of dress button-holes must be round, the stitches diverging like rays from the centre, and when you have worked the second side, thread the needle with the loose strand and pull it slightly, to straighten the edges; then fasten off, and close the button-hole with a straight bar of stitches across the other end, as in fig. 28.

Sewing on buttons (figs. 30 and 31). To sew linen or webbed buttons on to under-clothing, fasten in your thread with a stitch or two at the place where the button is to be; bring the needle out through the middle of the button, and make eight stitches, diverging from the

Fig. 30. Sewing on linen buttons   *Fig. 31. Sewing on webbed buttons*

centre like a star, and if you like, encircle them by a row of stitching, as in fig. 31. This done, bring the needle out between the stuff and the button, and twist the cotton six or seven times round it, then push the needle through to the wrong side, and fasten off.

Binding slits (figs. 32, 33, 34, 35). Nothing is more apt to tear than a slit whether it be hemmed or merely bound. To prevent this, make a semicircle of button-hole stitches at the bottom of the slit, and above that, to connect the two sides, a bridge of several threads covered with button-hole stitching.

In fig. 32 we show a hemmed slit, and in figs. 33 and 34 are two slits backed the one with a narrow, the other with a broad piece of the material cut on the cross.

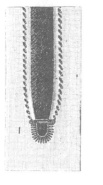 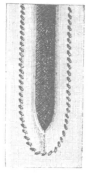  

Fig. 32. Binding slits with hem   *Fig. 33. Binding slits with piece on cross*   *Fig. 34. Binding slits with broad band*   *Fig. 35. Strengthening slits with gusset*

In under-linen, it often so happens that two selvedges meet at the slit, which renders binding unnecessary; in that case take a small square of stuff, turn in the raw edges, top-sew it into the slit on two sides, turn in the other two, fold over on the bias, and hem them down over the top-sewing, as shown in fig. 35. Such little squares of material, inserted into a slit or seam to prevent its tearing, are called gussets.

Sewing on piping (fig. 36). Piping is a border consisting of a cord or bobbin, folded into a strip of material cut on the cross, and affixed to the edge of an article to give it more strength and finish. It is a good substitute for a hem or binding on a bias edge, which by means of the cord can be held in, and prevented from stretching. Cut your strips diagonally across the web of the stuff, and very even; run them together, lay the cord or bobbin along the strip on the wrong side, 5 mm. from the edge, fold the edge over and tack the cord lightly in. Then lay it on the raw edge of the article, with the cord towards you, and with all the raw edges turned away from you. Back-stitch the piping to the edge, keeping close to the cord. Then turn the article round, fold in the raw outside edge over the others, and hem it down like an ordinary hem.

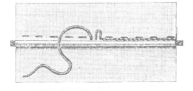

Fig. 36. Sewing on piping

Fixing whale-bones (fig. 37). Before slipping the whale-bone into its case or fold of stuff, pierce holes in it, top and bottom, with a red-hot stiletto. Through these holes make your stitches, diverging like rays or crossing each other as shown in fig. 37.

Herring-boning (fig. 38). This stitch is chiefly used for seams in flannel, and for over-casting dress-seams, and takes the place of hemming for fastening down the raw edges of a seam that has been run or stitched, without turning them in. Herring-boning is done from left to right, and forms two rows of stitches. Insert the needle from right to left, and make a stitch first above, and then below the edge, the threads crossing each other diagonally, as shown in fig. 38.

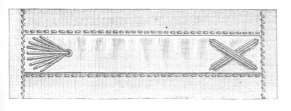

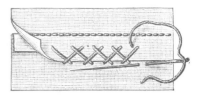

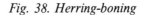

Fig. 37. Fixing whale-bones   *Fig. 38. Herring-boning*

Specimens of pattern darns

Mending

The mending of wearing apparel and house-linen, though often an ungrateful task is yet a very necessary one, to which every female hand ought to be carefully trained. How best to disguise and repair the wear and tear of use or accident is quite as valuable an art as that of making things new.

Under the head of mending, we include the strengthening and replacing of the worn and broken threads of a fabric, and the fitting in of new stuff in the place of that which is torn or damaged. The former is called darning, the latter, patching.

Darning. When only a few of the warp or woof (weft) threads are torn or missing, a darn will repair the mischief, provided the surrounding parts be sound. When the damage is more extensive the piece must be cut out.

In some cases the warp of the stuff itself can be used for darning, otherwise thread as much like the stuff as possible should be chosen.

Varieties of darning. These are four: (1) linen darning, (2) damask darning, (3) satin or twill darning, and (4) invisible darning, also called fine-drawing.

(1) **Linen darning** (figs. 39 and 40). All darns should be made on the wrong side of the stuff, excepting fig. 53, which it is sometimes better to make on the right side. The longitudinal running, to form the warp, must be made first. The thread must not be drawn tightly in running your stitches backwards and forwards, and be careful to leave loops at each turning, to allow for the shrinking of the thread in the washing, without its pulling the darn together.

Run your needle in about one cm. above the damaged part, take up one or two threads of the stuff and miss the same number, working straight to a thread; on reaching the hole, carry your cotton straight across it, take up alternate threads beyond, and proceed as before. Continue the rows backwards and forwards, taking up in each row the threads left in the preceding one. Turn the work round and do the same for the woof, alternately taking up and leaving the warp threads, where the cotton crosses the hole. The threads must lie so close both ways that the darn, when completed, replaces the original web. The threads are drawn far apart in the illustrations for the sake of clearness.

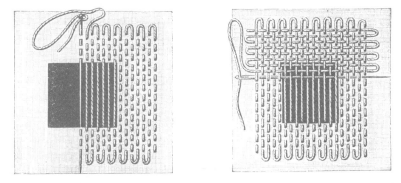

Fig. 39. Drawing in the warp threads.   *Fig. 40. Drawing in the woof threads.*

Diagonal linen darning (fig. 41). Darns are sometimes begun from the. corner, so as to form a diagonal web, but they are then much more visible than when they are worked straight to a thread, and therefore not advisable.

(2) **Satin or twill darning** (fig. 42). By twill darning, the damaged web of any twilled or diagonal material can be restored. It would be impossible to enumerate all the varieties of twilled stuffs, but the illustrations and accompanying directions will enable the worker to imitate them all.

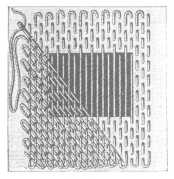 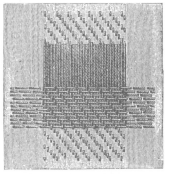

Fig. 41. Diagonal linen darning   *Fig. 42. Satin or twill darning*

Begin, as in ordinary darning, by running in the warp threads, then take up one thread and miss three. In every succeeding row advance one thread in the same direction. Or, miss one thread of the stuff and take up two, and as before advance one thread in the same direction every succeeding row. The order in which threads should be missed and taken up must depend on the web which the darn is intended to imitate.

When the original is a coloured stuff it is advisable to make a specimen darn first, on a larger scale, so that you may be more sure of obtaining a correct copy of the original web.

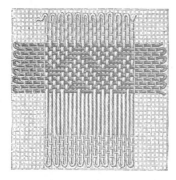

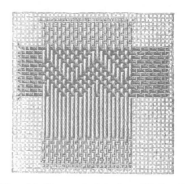

Fig. 43. Damask darning. Wrong side.   *Fig. 44. Damask darning. Right side.*

Fig. 45. Damask darning.   *Fig. 46. Damask darning*   *Fig. 47. Damask darning*
Covered ground.   *on needle-made ground*   *on needle-made ground*

(3) **Damask darning** (figs. 43, 44, 45, 46, 47, 48). A damask darn is begun in the same way as all other darns are; the pattern is formed by the cross-runnings and will vary with the number of warp threads taken up and missed in each successive running. The woven design which you are to copy with your needle must therefore be carefully examined first.

Figs. 43 and 44 show the wrong and right sides of a damask darn in process of being made.

Fig. 45 represents a completed one. In the case of coloured webs, a light shade of cotton is generally used for the warp and one that matches the stuff for the shot or woof.

Figs. 46 and 47 illustrate two specimens of darning, formerly done in the convents, from which it will be seen that the warp and the woof were first drawn in with rather fine thread and the pattern then worked into this foundation with coarser, or else coloured, thread.

Fig. 48, which is executed in two colours and is likewise copied from an old work on darning, shows the manner in which a dice-pattern is to be reproduced.

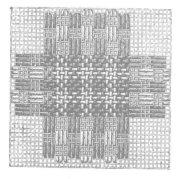

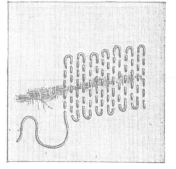

Fig. 48. Damask darning
with coloured thread

Fig. 49. Darning
lost in the ground

(4) **Darning lost in the ground** (fig. 49). A kind of darn used for repairing rents, the edges of which fit exactly into one another. Neither the torn threads of the material nor the rough edges must be cut off; the torn part is to be tacked upon another piece of cloth, wrong side uppermost, and the edges, drawn together by a thread, run in backwards and forwards across them. The stitches must be set as closely together as possible, and regularly inverted, as in every other darn. A much finer thread relatively than that of which the material is composed should in all cases be used for darning. In this instance also, for the sake of greater distinctness, the size of the thread has been magnified in the illustration.

Fine drawing (fig. 50). The art of making invisible darns in cloth, though such a useful one, is all but unknown. It is a tedious process and one which, though easy enough to understand, requires great care in the execution.

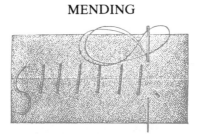

Fig. 50. Fine drawing

Use as fine a needle as possible and thread it with silk, or any other kind of fine fibre. Pare the edges of the rent on the right sides, quite clean and even, with a razor, so that both rent and stitches may be lost in the hairy surface of the cloth. Scissors do not cut so closely and are liable moreover to disturb the nap and render the darn more visible. When this is done, fit the edges exactly together and overcast them. Then thread a needle and slip it in, 2 or 3 mm. from the one edge and back again pointed towards you, through the other, so that neither needle nor thread are visible on either side. The stitches should be set slightly slanting and must be quite lost in the thickness of the cloth. The needle must always be put in exactly at the place where it came out, and the thread not be too tightly drawn.

When the darn is finished, lay the article on a bare table or ironing-board, cover it with a damp cloth, and iron it. The sharpest eye will fail to detect a rent when carefully darned in this manner.

Patching. As we have already said, when the defective part is past darning it must be cut out and a new piece of stuff inserted in its place. If the garment be no longer new, it should be patched with a lighter material than that of which it was originally made. The patch should be of the same shape, and cut the same way of the stuff, as the piece it is to replace; it should also be just so much larger as to allow for the turnings in, and can either be top-sewn, or else run and felled in.

Back-stitching and felling in a patch (fig. 51). Tack in the new piece so that its edges overlap the edges of the hole. The back-stitching must be done on the article itself as this renders it easier to do the corners neatly. The hem is turned down on to the patch. Make a little snip at the corners with your scissors to prevent puckering. The back-stitching should form a right angle at each corner.

Top-sewing in a patch (fig. 52). To do this, the edges of the hole and of the patch must first be turned in and either over-cast or hemmed to prevent their fraying, after which sew the two edges together. The raw

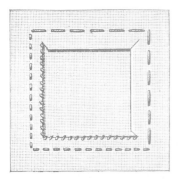

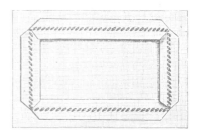

Fig. 52. Top-sewing in a patch

Fig. 51. Back-stitching and
felling in a patch

edges may also be turned in with herring-boning as in fig. 38, putting
the needle only through one layer of stuff.

Drawing in a patch (fig. 53). Take a square piece of the original stuff, 5
or 6 cm. larger each way than the hole it is to fill, draw out threads on
all the four sides till the piece exactly matches the hole and tack it into
its place. Thread a very fine needle with the two ends of a thread of silk
or another fine thread, run it in at the corner of the stuff and draw it
out, leaving a loop behind. Into this loop slip the first of the threads
which, as it were, form a fringe to the patch and tighten the loop
around it, and so on with each thread, alternately taking up and
leaving threads in the stuff, as in ordinary darning.

To put a patch into a thin material in this manner, you must darn in
the threads a good long way into the material in order that the double
layer of threads may be less visible.

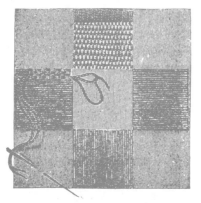

Fig. 53. Drawing in a patch

27

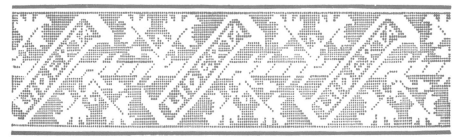

Strip of cut open-work on white linen

Single & Cut Open-work

The above heading comprises every sort of needlework to which the drawing out of threads is a preliminary. By sewing over the single threads that remain and drawing them together in different ways an infinite variety of patterns can be produced. Many pretty combinations, also, can be made of open-work, cross-stitch, and other kinds of embroidery.

The two different kinds of open-work. One is called single open-work, the Italian *Punto tirato*, in which the first step is to draw out one layer of threads; the other, cut open-work, the Italian *Punto tagliato*, for which both the warp and the woof threads have to be drawn out.

Single open-work (Punto tirato). This, in its simplest form, is the ornamental latticed hem, in common use where something rather more decorative than an ordinary hem (fig. 7) is required, and consists in drawing out one layer of threads, either the warp or the woof.

Single hem-stitch (fig. 54). Draw out, according to the coarseness of the stuff, two or four threads, below the edge of the turning, and tack your hem down to the line thus drawn. Fasten your thread in to the left, and work your hem from right to left, taking up three or four cross-threads at a time, and inserting your needle immediately above into the folded hem, three or four threads from the edge, and then drawing it out.

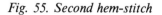

Fig. 54. Single hem-stitch   *Fig. 55. Second hem-stitch*

28

Second hem-stitch (fig. 55). Prepare your hem as for fig. 54 and work from left to right with this difference, that after drawing two or three cross-threads together, from right to left, you skip the same number of perpendicular threads you took up below, and insert your needle downwards from above, bringing it out at the bottom edge of the hem. These stitches can be used for the right side also.

Ladder stitch hem (fig. 56). Complete the hem as already directed in fig. 54, then draw out three or five threads more, turn the work round, and repeat the process, taking up the same clusters of threads which you took up in the first row of stitches, thus forming little perpendicular bars.

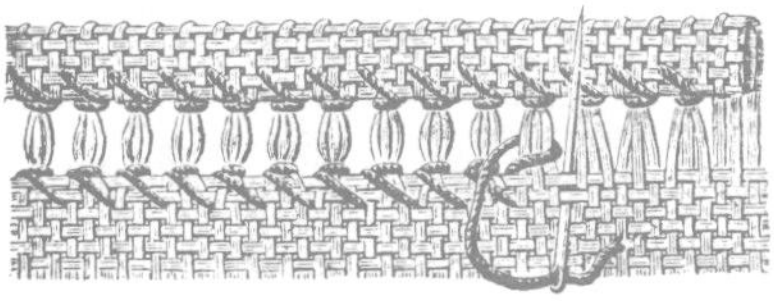

Fig. 56. Ladder stitch hem

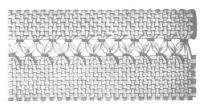

Fig. 57. Double hem-stitch

Double hem-stitch (fig. 57). Begin as in fig. 54, forming your clusters of an even number of threads and then, in making your second row of stitches, draw half the threads of one cluster and half of the next together, thereby making them slant, first one way and then the other.

Antique hem-stitch (figs. 58 and 59). In the old, elaborate, linen needlework we often meet with two kinds of hem-stitching, seldom found in modern books on needlework. Figs. 58 to 61 are magnified representations of the same. At the necessary depth for forming a narrow hem a thread is drawn, except in the case of very fine textures, where the edge is rolled, not laid; then fasten in the working thread at the left and work the stitches from left to right. Passing your needle from right to left, under three or four threads, draw the thread round the cluster and carry your needle on, through as many threads of the upper layer of stuff as you took up below, so that the stitch may always emerge from the middle of the cluster.

Fig. 58. Antique hem-stitch, wrong side. 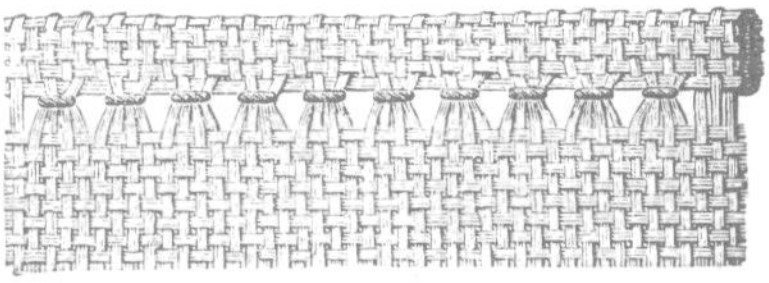   *Fig. 59. Antique hem-stitch, right side.*

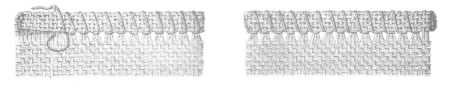

Fig. 60. Antique hem-stitch, wrong side.   *Fig. 61. Antique hem-stitch, right side.*

Antique hem-stitch (figs. 60 and 61). These show the right and wrong sides of the hem; here the rolled hem is prepared as above, but the stitches are worked from right to left, and the thread is carried round the little roll so that, as shown in fig. 61, it is visible on both sides of the hem. The needle does not enter the stuff but is carried back at once, from the outside, and put in again between two clusters of threads.

Fig. 62. Slanting hem-stitch, wrong side.   *Fig. 63. Slanting hem-stitch, right side.*

Slanting hem-stitch (figs. 62 and 63). Bring out your needle and thread two or three threads above the edge of the turning, between the first and second of the three cross-threads that compose the cluster, and then slip it under the cluster, from right to left. The loop must lie in front of the needle. When you have drawn up the stitch, put the needle in one thread further on, and take up two threads. Fig. 63 shows the stitch on the right side.

Double-rowed ornamental seam (figs. 64, 65, 66). Begin with any one of the hems already described then, counting as many threads downwards as are clustered together in the first row, draw out a second thread and cluster the perpendicular threads in this second line together, as shown in figs. 64 and 65. On the right side the stitch is straight (fig. 66). Coloured cottons should be used for all the above patterns of hem-stitch when they are to be introduced into coloured embroideries.

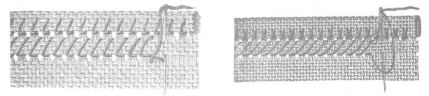

Fig. 64. Fig. 65. Double-rowed ornamental seam, wrong side.

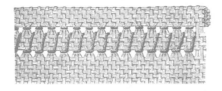

Fig. 66. Double-rowed ornamental seam, right side.

Single three-rowed open-work (fig. 67). This, and the following patterns, are suitable for the headings of hems, and for connecting strips of embroidery, and are also often used instead of lace and lace insertion.

Fig. 67 will be found specially useful in cases where the object is to produce a good deal of effect, at the cost of as little labour as possible. Make six rows of hem-stitching, as in fig. 64. The first and sixth rows serve as a finish, above and below. The second and third are worked after drawing out six threads, the fourth and fifth after drawing out eight. The clusters must all consist of an even number of threads. The upper and lower band of open-work is to be copied from fig. 57, the centre one from fig. 56. Divide the threads of the perpendicular clusters in two; insert the needle from left to right underneath half the second cluster, turn the needle's eye, by a second movement, from left to right, and take up the second part of the first cluster, drawing it under and in front of the first half of the second cluster. Be careful not to draw your thread too tightly.

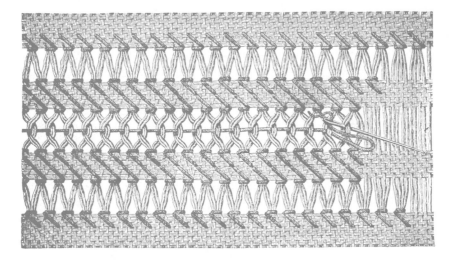

Fig. 67. Single three-rowed open-work

31

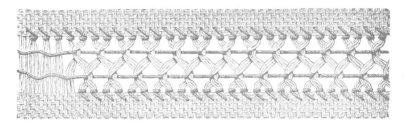

Fig. 68. Open-work with two threads drawn through

Open-work with two threads drawn through (fig. 68). One such wide lane of open-work between two finishing rows of stitches may have two threads drawn through it.

Open-work with three threads drawn through (fig. 69). Overcast both edges with single stitches; draw the clusters together in the middle, as in fig. 67, then above and below the middle thread draw in first one thread and then a second, straight above it, securing the latter with back-stitches to enclose the clusters between two threads.

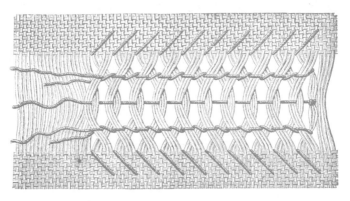

Fig. 69. Open-work with three threads drawn through

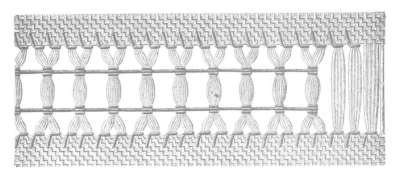
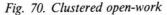

Fig. 70. Clustered open-work

Clustered open-work (fig. 70). Draw out from sixteen to eighteen threads between two hem-stitched edges. Fasten your thread in 3 mm. above the seam-edge, and wind it three times round every two clusters, passing the needle the third time under the first two rounds to fasten the thread. The thread, thus drawn through, must be left rather slack. A second row of stitches similar to the first and at the same distance from the bottom edge completes this pattern. To give it greater strength, you may if you like work back over the first thread with a second, taking care to pass it under the knot which was formed by the first.

Double-rowed cluster open-work (fig. 71). A very good effect can be obtained by making the above stitch in such a manner as to form groups of three clusters each, between hem-stitched bands of the stuff.

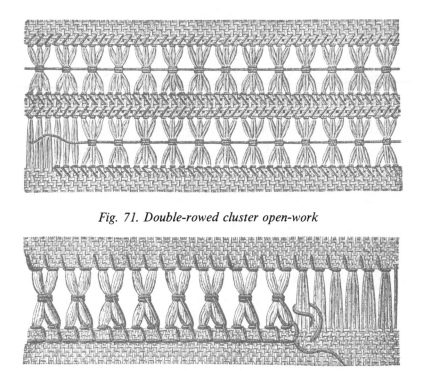

Fig. 71. Double-rowed cluster open-work

Fig. 72. Turkish cluster open-work

Turkish cluster open-work (fig. 72). After portioning off and sewing up the clusters on one side, draw out twelve or fourteen threads and make your connecting-stitch and hem, all in one, as follows: bring out the thread before the cluster and pass it round it, from right to left, over three horizontal and under four perpendicular threads, again from left to right, over the four threads just passed over, and out at the second cluster; laying it over this, you bring it out behind the first cluster, wind it round the middle of them both, and pass it through, between the over-casting stitches, back to the hem; encircle the second cluster with a loop-stitch, and carry your thread again over three horizontal and four perpendicular threads, and upwards, slanting underneath the stuff, out in front of the next cluster.

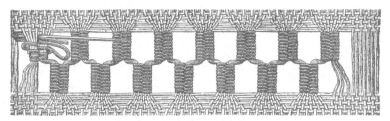

Fig. 73. Open-work with needleweaving

Open work with needleweaving (fig 73). Draw out from eight to twelve threads, according to the quality of the stuff. Insert your needle and thread between two clusters and pass it, as if you were darning, backwards and forwards over them until they are encased half way down with stitches. In doing so, work with the eye of the needle forward and the point towards your thimble. To pass to the next cluster, take one stitch back, under the one just darned, and bring your thread underneath the threads of the stuff to the second cluster.

Open-work in three colours (fig. 74). This pattern, which is to be done in the same way as fig. 73, requires the drawing out of at least eighteen threads. Every cross-line of three clusters is to be worked in one colour. The colours may all be different, or you may if you prefer take three shades of the same colour.

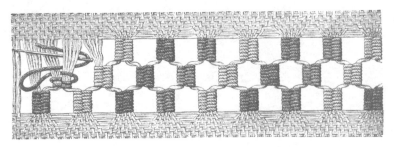

Fig. 74. Open-work in three colours.
Colours: DMC 311 blue, 355 brown, 352 geranium.

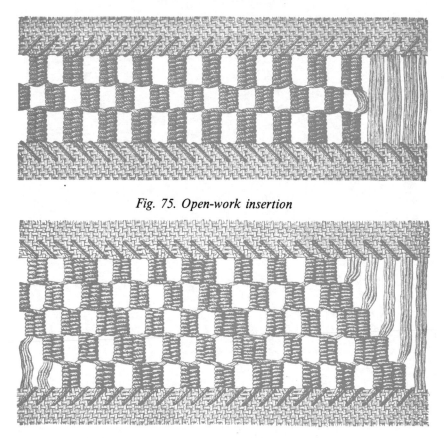

Fig. 75. Open-work insertion

Fig. 76. Open-work insertion

Open-work insertion (figs. 75 and 76). For both these the edges are to be overcast and the needleweaving packed sufficiently closely together for the threads of the stuff to be entirely covered.

Fig. 75 requires the drawing out of eighteen threads, fig. 76 of thirty. Both admit of several colours being used.

Open-work insertion (fig. 77). After drawing out sixteen or eighteen threads, bind both sides with stitches made over four horizontal and four perpendicular threads as follows: make one back-stitch over four disengaged threads, then bring up your thread from right to left over four horizontal and under four perpendicular threads, back over the four last threads, and draw it out beside the next cluster. The clusters, as they now stand, are bound together in the middle, three by three, with needleweaving. The thread must be fastened in and cut off after each group is finished.

35

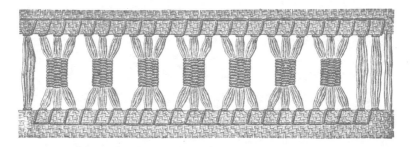

Fig. 77. Open-work insertion

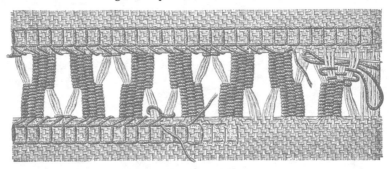

Fig. 78. Open-work insertion

Open-work insertion (fig. 78). First bind the two edges with stitches in the ordinary way. At the last stitch introduce the thread slanting, according to the dotted line, pass it under four horizontal and three perpendicular threads of the stuff and draw it out; then over three threads from right to left, and back under the same, from left to right, and out again; over four horizontal threads, and under and again over three perpendicular ones; for the next stitch, you again follow the dotted slanting line.

Then make the needleweaving over nine threads, or three clusters. At half their length, leave out three threads, first on the right, then on the left, whilst in the other half, in a similar manner, take in three; so that you have two darned and two undarned clusters standing opposite each other. Finally, you overcast the single clusters and connect every two with a lock-stitch, as shown in the accompanying illustration.

Open-work insertion (fig. 79). Draw out twenty threads, overcast both edges with stitches made over three threads. Then make slanting stitches proceeding out from these over three, six and nine threads respectively, all three terminating in a perpendicular line, one below the other.

For the open-work, twist the thread five times quite tightly round and round one cluster, bring it to the edge between the second and third clusters, and connect these by means of six rows of needleweaving to and fro: join the first and second clusters in the same way by twelve stitches and finish by twisting the thread five times round the remaining length of the first cluster. The second half of the open-work figure is carried out in a similar manner over the third and fourth clusters.

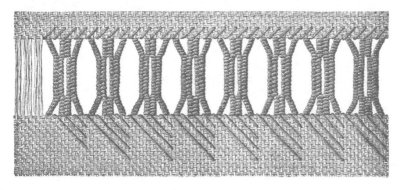

Fig. 79. Open-work insertion

Open-work insertion in four colours (fig. 80). Draw out from twenty-five to thirty threads. The outside figures are executed over six clusters of three threads each, in a dark and light shade alternately of the same colour. Each of the middle figures combines three clusters of the two figures above it and may be executed either in a different colour altogether or in a lighter shade of the one employed in the top row. The little star in the centre should be worked in dark red, or black.

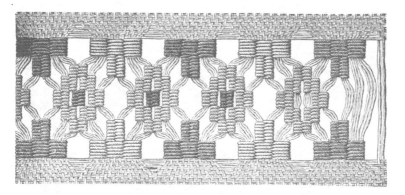

Fig. 80. Open-work insertion in four colours.
Colours: DMC 899 and 326 Turkish reds, 322 and 823 indigo blues.

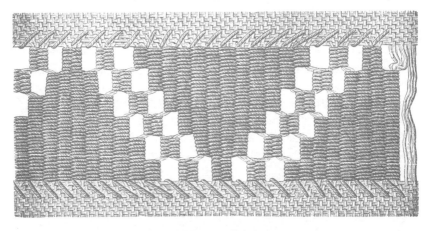

Fig. 81. Open-work insertion

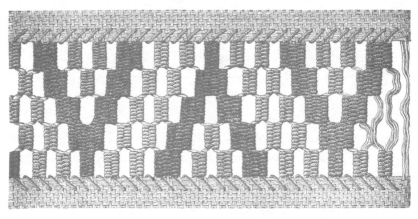

Fig. 82. Open-work insertion

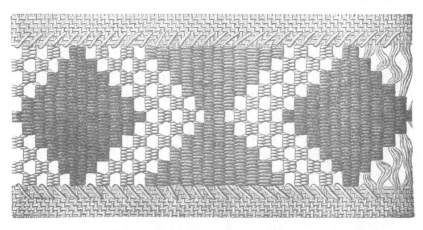

Fig. 83. Open-work insertion

Open-work insertions (figs. 81, 82, 83). For each of these draw out forty threads. Fig. 81 worked in white and one colour, say, red, comprises fourteen clusters of four threads each. Begin at the top of the big pyramid so that the threads which you run in can be more closely crowded together.

In fig. 82, the two rows of short clusters are worked in three colours, one for the pyramid of steps, one for the inner spaces and one for the diagonal steps between pyramids.

Fig. 83 also is to be worked in three colours, one for the diamonds, one for the joined-triangle shapes and one for the diagonal steps between. Each figure contains eighteen clusters, of three threads each.

Open-work insertion with spiders (fig. 84). The edges are to be herring-boned, as described in fig. 38. In the middle, the so-called spiders are made over every group of four clusters. The thread that runs out from the spider passes over two clusters and under one and then three or four times over and under the clusters, as in darning, and so back under the spider at the place at which it was drawn in, and then on to the next four strands of thread.

Fig. 84. Open-work insertion with spiders

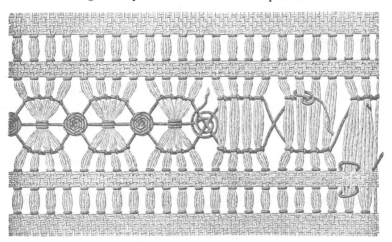

Fig. 85. Three-rowed open-work

Three-rowed open-work (fig. 85). Draw out five threads for the narrow strip and from fourteen to sixteen for the wide one. Each cluster should consist of four threads. The narrow bands between are to be herring-boned on either side. The dotted line shows the course of the thread on the wrong side. Then unite each separate cluster in the middle with a back-stitch, as shown in the illustration, and finally join every group of four clusters together, with three stitches, and make a spider in the middle of the open-work at the point where the threads intersect each other.

Fig. 86. Open-work insertion with rings

Open-work insertion with rings (fig. 86). Bind the edges on both sides with straight, two-sided, stitches. Draw out from twenty-four to thirty threads. Wind your thread six or seven times round the middle of each cluster of nine threads and then make needleweaving, above and below, to a length of 3 mm. When you have completed two clusters join them together by four interlocked stitches; wind your thread three times round the single thread, and sew it over with close stitches.

Open-work insertion with spiders (fig. 87). Draw out twenty-four threads. Ornament the two edges with half-spiders. You begin these over two threads, and go on taking in others, to the number of eight. The whole spider in the middle is made as described above.

Open-work insertion (figs. 88 and 89). The beauty of this otherwise simple pattern lies in the peculiar knot with which the edges of the stuff are ornamented.

Carry the working thread, as shown in fig. 89, from right to left, over and under four threads; then bring the needle back under the thread which lies slanting, form a loop with the forefinger of the left

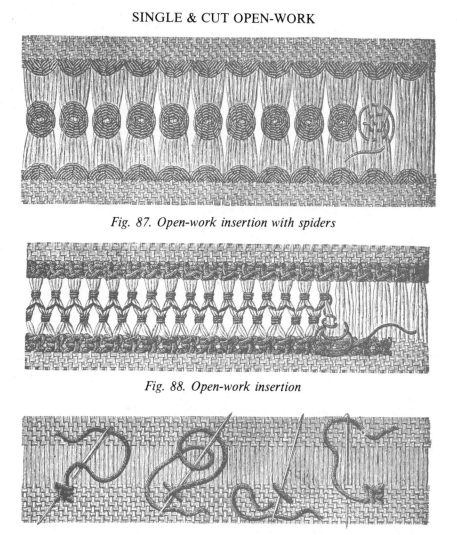

Fig. 87. Open-work insertion with spiders

Fig. 88. Open-work insertion

Fig. 89. Explanation of the stitch for fig. 88

hand, slip it on to the needle, and draw it up close to the first stitch; pull the needle through the knot, and proceed to the next stitch.

Fig. 88 explains how the open-work in the middle should be carried out.

Open-work with binding stitch (fig. 90). For this pattern, which is a very laborious one to work, draw out twenty-eight threads. Bind the edges with two-sided stitches over two, three, four and five threads respectively. For the middle figures, you must reckon four threads for the clusters, round which the working thread is tightly twisted, eight for the darned clusters, ornamented with picots and sixteen for the rectangular rosettes, in two colours.

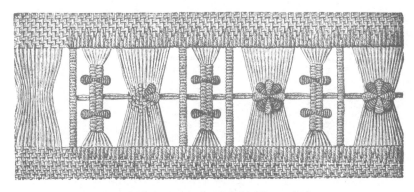

Fig. 90. Open-work with binding stitch

Make a loose spider over the threads as a background for the rosette. Work the picots in a different colour from the cluster and the rosettes, likewise, in two colours. The connecting loops between the figures should be made as you go along, the thread being always carried back into the loop just made.

Cutting out threads at the corners (figs 91, 92, 93, 94). If you want to carry a latticed-hem or a simple open-work pattern round a corner, you must cut and loosen the threads on both sides about one cm. from the edge of the hem, as seen in fig. 91. The loose threads can be pushed into the turning, and the edge button-holed, as in fig. 92.

If, on the other hand, the stitching be continued without interruption, as indicated in the upper part of fig. 93, the loose threads must be brought to the wrong side and, as represented in the lower part of fig. 93, fastened down with a few stitches.

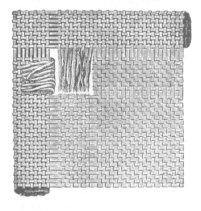

Fig. 91. The cutting and loosening of the threads at the corners

Fig. 92. The overcasting of the disengaged edge at the corner, the threads being turned in within the hem.

42

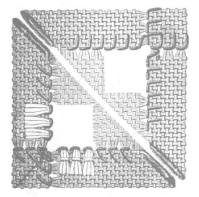

Fig. 93. Bordering the disengaged
edge with hem-stitching, the threads
being turned over.

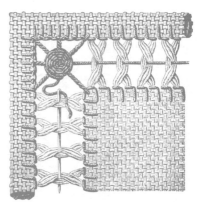

Fig. 94. Filling in the corner
with a spider, and continuation
of the lattice-work.

Cut open-work (Punto tagliato). For cut open-work, threads have to be drawn out both ways, the number of threads withdrawn to depend on the pattern. Threads left between others that have been cut out serve as a foundation on which a great variety of stitches can be worked. Evenweave fabrics, with clearly seen and similarly sized warp and woof threads, should be chosen for all cut open-work, for then the empty spaces that remain after threads have been drawn out both ways will be perfectly square.

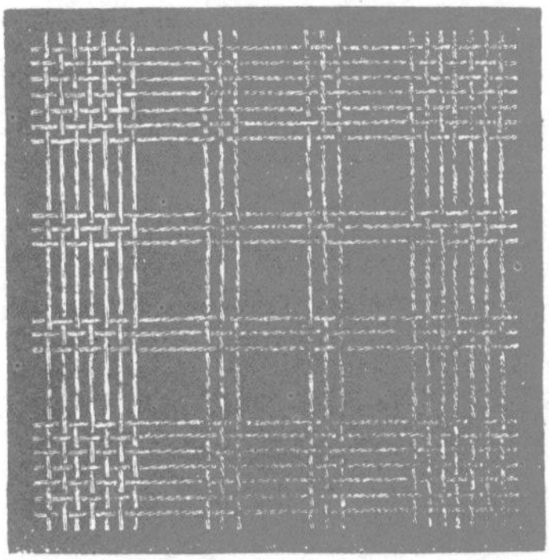

Fig. 95. Drawing out threads both
ways, without regard to the edges.

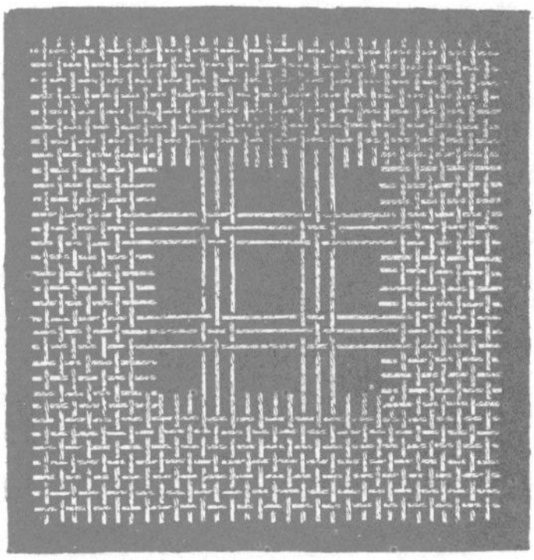

Fig. 96. Cutting out threads
in the middle of the stuff

Drawing out threads both ways (fig. 95). The same number of threads must be drawn out each way; most patterns require the same number of threads to be left as are drawn out. In fig. 95, three threads have been drawn out and three left.

Cutting out threads (fig. 96). We often meet with cut open-work

 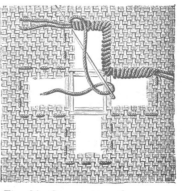

Fig. 97. Button-holing the raw   *Fig. 98. Overcasting the raw*
edges of cut open-work   *edges of cut open-work*

patterns set in another kind of embroidery. In such cases, the threads that are to be cut out must be cut a few millimetres within the edge and then drawn out so that there may be a frame of the stuff left intact outside.

Button-holing the raw edges (fig. 97). In very fine linen textures the threads can simply be cut out, but in the case of coarser stuffs, and when a pattern ends in steps as in figs. 102, 103, 104, the raw edges must be button-holed as in fig. 97.

Overcasting the raw edges (fig. 98). Cording the raw edges is even better than button-holing them. Count the number of threads that have to be cut out, run in a thread to mark the pattern and then cut the threads through, not less than two threads within the line.

Overcasting the trellised ground (fig. 99). If you only have a small surface to embroider you can draw out all the threads at once. In the case of a large piece of work it is better to begin by removing the threads in one direction only and completing all the little bars one way

Fig. 99. Overcasting the trellised ground

first, after which you draw out the threads the other way and embroider those you leave. In this way you will secure greater equality and finish in your work.

Ground for square, fig. 104 (figs. 100 and 101). Alternate horizontal and vertical clusters are bound in the usual way. Along every other horizontal row, halfway along a bar, carry the thread over two bars and back *(a)*. Work two-bars-on and two-bars-off in this manner, as illustrated. Similarly, when working every other vertical row, carry threads over two bars (from *b* and back again).

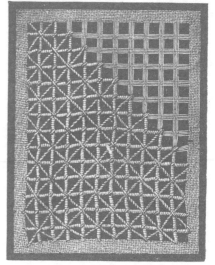

Fig. 100. Lattice-ground for square in fig. 104, showing the course of the stitches.

Fig. 101. Lattice-ground for square in fig. 104.

In fig. 101, overcast both ways first and then fill in the ground with interlaced threads worked row by row, throwing the thread from one square to the other as you go, and doubling it as you return.

Lattice-ground and damask stitch for square, fig. 104 (fig. 102). Our illustration shows a third kind of open-work ground with one corner in damask stitch, of the square represented in fig. 104. The little bars which intersect each square crossways are formed as those in fig. 100 only that with each row of horizontal (and vertical) clusters being bound halfway across (or down) every alternate bar the thread is thrown across to the next bar. The damask stitches are described in the next chapter.

Lattice-ground and damask stitches for square, fig. 104 (fig. 103) Damask, or gobelin stitches, are given in figs. 151, 152, 153. The

Fig. 102. Lattice-ground with a portion of square, fig. 104.

Fig. 103. Lattice-ground and damask stitch for square, fig. 104.

ground of this part of the square (fig. 103) is adorned with narrow bars formed as follows. After binding horizontal and vertical bars, twice throw diagonal threads from every alternate junction so that all diagonal bars are formed of pairs of threads. You then weave in and out (over left thread, under right, over right, under left) to produce needleweaving.

Quarter of the square in single and cut open-work, and damask-stitch (fig. 104). Original size 48 cm. square. This handsome square is worked in unbleached cotton on a white ground; it may also be worked in colours. A very good effect is produced by using red, blue or green for the damask stitch, and a uniform pale tint for the cut open-work.

Figs. 100, 101, 102, 103 illustrate details of the square, which is represented here one third of the original size. The centre piece (fig. 102) is bordered by four stripes, two long and two short, the former

Fig. 104. Quarter of the square in single and cut open-work, and damask stitch. Original size 48 cm. square.

containing two lozenge-shaped open-work figures, separated and finished off by damask stitches; the latter, only one such figure. For the insertion in single open-work, that recurs three times, you will find a variety of designs in figs. 80, 81, 82, 83, 86, 87.

Drawing in the pattern (fig. 105). *Darning* in the threads is a slower process and one that requires greater skill than *drawing* them in. The illustration shows the proper order and direction of the stitches for fig. 107. Generally all bound bars should be formed before the actual pattern is filled in.

Darning in the threads (fig. 106). In old needlework we often find the pattern reserved, that is, left blank and outlined by the grounding. As it is difficult, especially in executing minute and delicate figures, to withdraw the threads partially without injuring the linen foundation, they are withdrawn throughout and new ones drawn in to form the pattern. To explain this more clearly, the original threads of the material are represented in a lighter shade than the new ones that are drawn in; the course of the stitches is indicated in a darker shade.

Broad insertion in cut open-work, with the pattern drawn in (fig. 107). This insertion, suitable according to the foundation it is worked on

Fig. 105. Drawing in the pattern   *Fig. 106. Darning in the threads*
(explanation of fig. 107)   *(explanation of fig. 108)*

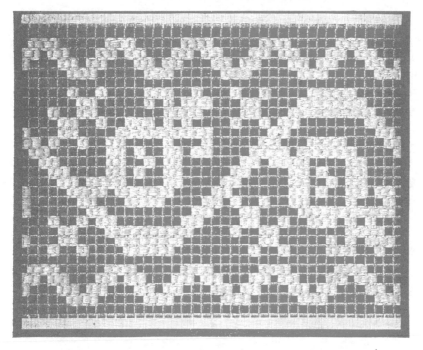

Fig. 107. Broad insertion in cut open-work, with pattern drawn in.

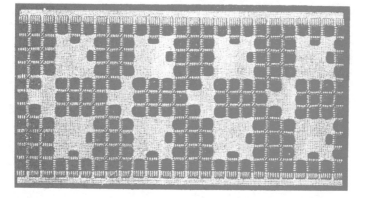

Fig. 108. Insertion in cut open-work, with pattern darned in.

for the decoration of curtains, table-covers, bed-linen or under-clothing, is made as shown in fig. 105. If intended for decoration of any article made of white linen, we recommend unbleached materials for the lattice-work and bleached for the pattern, to bring it out in strong relief.

Insertion in cut open-work, with pattern darned in (fig. 108). This insertion can be introduced into any kind of linen material, and used

49

for ornamenting towels, aprons, bed-linen and table-linen. When it is used to connect bands of cross-stitch embroidery, the open-work should be of the same colour as the embroidery and the pattern worked in white or unbleached cotton to correspond with the foundation. In fig. 108, the pattern is half as large again as in the original.

Cut open-work pattern (figs. 109 and 110). This pattern, more of the nature of lace than any pattern already shown, is well adapted for trimming not only household articles but also church furniture, altar-cloths and the like.

Fig. 109, a magnified representation of the work in process of execution, shows ten threads withdrawn each way and six left, with open spaces between. The arcs (upper part of illustration) are worked over three carefully laid threads, carried across from the middle of one

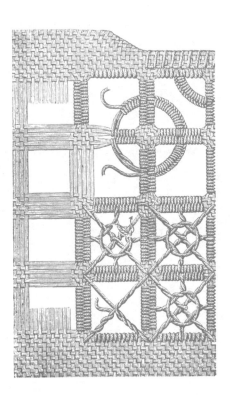

Fig. 109. Cut open-work pattern:
fig. 110 in process of execution.

Fig. 110. Cut open-work pattern

bar to the middle of the bar at right angles to it. The wheels (lower part of illustration), on the other hand, are begun and finished at the same corner. Overcast the cut edges, and hem-stitch the outside layer of stuff (figs. 60 and 61).

Greek cut open-work pattern (fig. 111). After the foregoing explanations, no difficulty will be found in copying the beautiful Greek cut open-work pattern illustrated in fig. 111. Here the main block of the design is formed of 48 warp and weft threads withdrawn and three threads then darned as described above, forming needlewoven bars. The narrower patterns along the top and bottom of the illustration are formed of 21 threads withdrawn each way. The cut edges, from bar to bar, are hem-stitched on both sides, leaving four threads of the stuff between.

The long bars, in the second figure, are button-holed on both sides, those with the picots, on one side only.

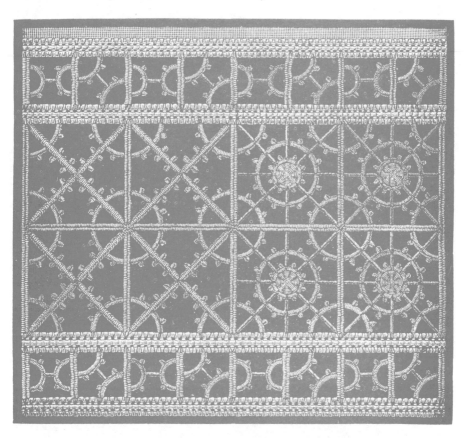

Fig. 111. Greek cut open-work pattern

Net strip in imitation of Brussels Lace

Net and Damask Stitches

Many net embroidery patterns and damask patterns consist of a combination of ordinary running and darning stitches. Others include chain, stem and cross-stitch.

Net embroidery. All these kinds of stitches can be worked on coarse net as well as on the finest quality of real Brussels net.

Tracing with running-stitches (fig. 112). Have your pattern traced on linen or paper; tack the net upon it, and copy it carefully on the net with running-stitches. As in darning, the stitches must run first above and then beneath, alternating in each succeeding row. At the turn of the lines, the stitches cross each other, as shown in the illustration.

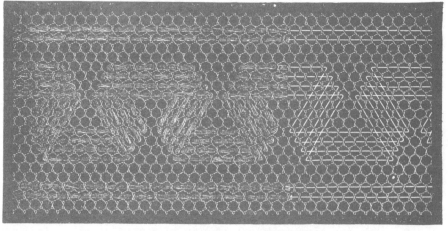

Fig. 112. Tracing with running-stitches

Net pattern (fig. 113). Here too the pattern is traced with running stitches which are run in on both sides of each row of meshes. The thread is carried first to the right and then to the left under every alternate bar of the net and out again. Between the first and second rows, one thread of the foundation must be left uncovered. In the next row the thread is carried back again so that it encircles each mesh. In the third row the thread passes under the same bar of net as in the second, the threads touching each other. The fourth row is a repetition of the first.

Net pattern (fig. 114). This consists of two rows of stitches. In the first, the single stitches run diagonally from left to right, over and under a mesh; in the second row the triple stitches, also carried diagonally across a mesh, lie from right to left.

Fig. 113 *Fig. 114*

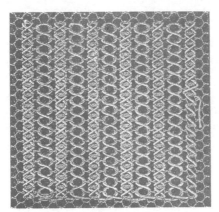

Fig. 115   Net patterns

Net pattern (fig. 115). Begin with a double row, as in fig. 113; this is followed by a row of cross-stitch, touching the others, for which the

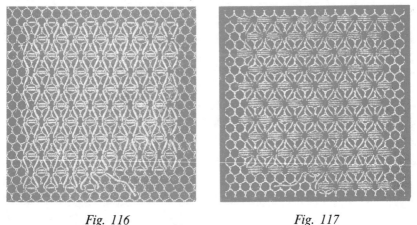

Fig. 116
        Net patterns
                        Fig. 117

thread has to be carried first under one of the straight bars of the mesh and then diagonally across it. A second, similar row of stitches backwards completes the crosses. This can be further varied by the introduction of a row of triple stitches, after the double row, as in fig. 114, and the repetition of the two first only.

These rows can also be worked in two colours or in white thread and washing gold.

Net pattern (fig. 116). Begin at the top, carrying the thread first under and then over two bars and a mesh, and then underneath as before. In the second, as in the first row, the threads must be drawn in, so that 4 threads always meet in one mesh and two run parallel to each other through the same mesh.

Net pattern (fig. 117). This pattern, which resembles fig. 116 in the execution, is thickened by laid stitches worked three times in the same holes and connected, block to block, by single diagonal stitches.

Very pretty varieties are to be obtained by the introduction of several colours. Take white, for instance, for the first row and different shades of the same colour for the second, third, fourth and fifth rows.

Net pattern (fig. 118). After one row of cross-stitch, such as was described in fig. 115, add a second, carrying the thread under the bar that lies between the first stitches so that the two rows only cover three threads of the net. The close bands of cross-stitch must be divided from each other by one row of net bars.

Net pattern (fig. 119). First work four vertical stitches over one mesh and two bars. After the fourth stitch, the thread is carried forward

54

under two bars to the next group. The holes between these stitches are then filled by two double vertical rows of darning stitches. Here you may introduce a variety in the colour, using either white and unbleached, or unbleached and pale blue, or some other combination of the kind.

Net pattern (fig. 120). Make three diagonal stitches over three bars and two meshes then, returning to the mesh out of which the first stitches come, make three more in the opposite direction. In the second row, the stitches meet in the same mesh as those of the first.

Net pattern (fig. 121). Carry the thread upwards from below, over a bar of the net, then pass it horizontally under another bar and carrying it downwards, pass it under a diagonal bar and then horizontally over three vertical bars. In the second row, your loops must be turned the opposite way. When the whole foundation is

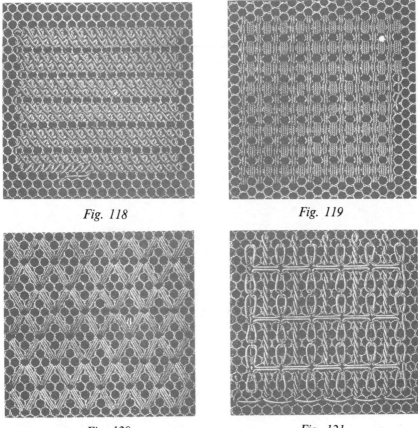

Fig. 118

Fig. 119

Fig. 120

Fig. 121

Net patterns

finished, run a thread vertically over the whole surface and overcast it. A good effect is produced by using white and unbleached cottons, in alternate rows.

Net pattern (fig. 122). This pattern consists of one row of overcasting, one of stitches like those described in fig. 113, and one of cross-stitch, as in fig. 38, running diagonally across the stuff.

Net pattern (fig. 123). Three kinds of stitches are required for this pattern. In the first vertical row the stitch lies crossed underneath the net. In the second, 3 vertical stitches are made over one mesh, the first and the last of which are carried across three meshes. In the third row, button-hole stitches are carried from right to left over two diagonal bars, in such a manner that the thread is drawn through the mesh facing the loops, and the next stitch comes out under the loop of the preceding one.

Net pattern (fig. 124). Fill in every other diagonal row of meshes with chain stitch, inserting the needle into the same mesh it came out of, so that the thread lies in front of the needle in a loop. The rows of chain stitch may be made with two or three rows of meshes between them. Even the diagonal lines by themselves make a very pretty foundation for other stitches.

Net pattern (fig. 125). The first row, worked from left to right, consists of three loop stitches upwards and three downwards, each over one bar. In the second row, divided from the first by one row of stitches, the inner loops must be turned towards each other; in the third, the outer ones. Any of the stitches already described can be introduced into this pattern to enliven it.

Net insertions (figs. 126 and 127). These two, as well as the subsequent patterns, are mostly worked in darning stitch and simple overcasting.

The scallops in fig. 126 are formed of darning stitches, over 4, 3, 2 and 1 mesh respectively. In the intervening space, which is five meshes wide, the stitch shown in fig. 117 may be introduced.

In repeating the pattern, the stitches forming the scallops must be made to run in the opposite direction. Instead of the thread simply drawn through the middle, little stars like those described in fig. 133, have a very pretty effect.

In fig. 127, the thread is first carried round one mesh and then on to the next scallop. In the second scallop, which turns the opposite way, the thread is carried once more round the last mesh after the pyramid is completed and then on to the next figure.

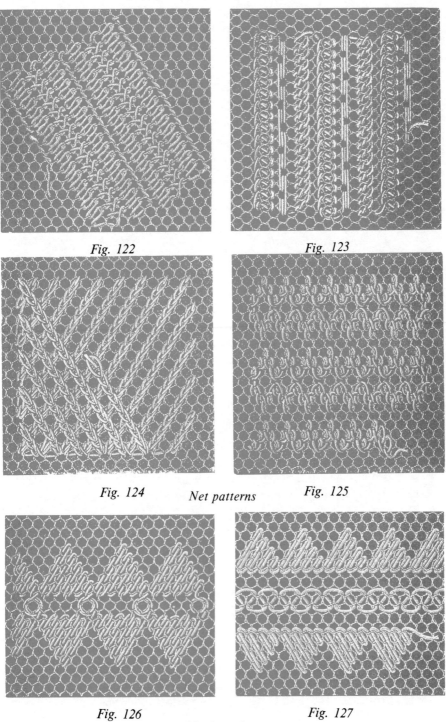

Fig. 122   Fig. 123

Fig. 124   *Net patterns*   Fig. 125

Fig. 126   Fig. 127

Net insertions

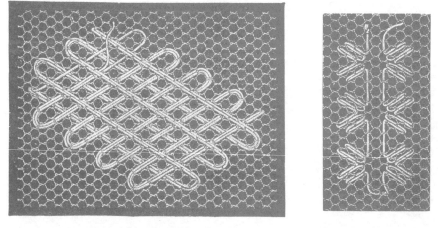

Fig. 128. Net pattern

Fig. 129. Net insertion

Net pattern (fig. 128). This checked pattern is also worked in darning stitch. Carry pairs of threads through every second row of meshes. When one set of diagonals is finished, the upper ones are worked across them in the same way. Here the stitches may, if preferred, be distributed more sparingly: if they are set wider apart, the spaces between should be filled up in some way. Little dots will answer the purpose best.

Net insertions (figs. 129, 130, 131). These three patterns are specially suitable for insertions, neck-tie lappets and the like, in the place of crochet, pillow, and other kinds of lace. Both design and stitch are clearly enough represented in the relevant figures for further explanation to be unnecessary. All three should be worked with rather coarse cotton, and Soutache (braid) drawn in produces an excellent effect.

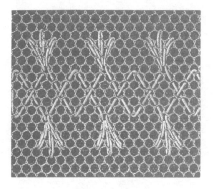

Fig. 130. Net insertion

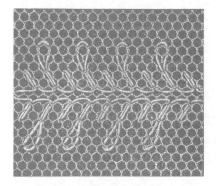

Fig. 131. Net insertion

Net pattern (fig. 132). These delicate little figures can be worked into either a close pattern or can be strewn singly over the surface. The closer you set the stitches, the more clear and distinct the stars will be. The thread must be drawn into the centre mesh from without, so as to be invisible if possible, and then back again to the outside when the stitches are finished.

Net pattern (fig. 133). These flowerets have a very pretty effect, set either singly, or in double or triple rows, and are very useful for filling up gaps or supplementing rows.

Net pattern (fig. 134). These star-shaped figures, their longest stitch covering three straight bars and two meshes, and the shortest three diagonal bars and two meshes, may, like the above flowerets, be ranged closely together in rows, so that two horizontal and two vertical stitches meet in one mesh. Cottons of two colours should be used in order that the figures may be distinct from each other.

Fig. 132

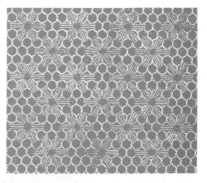

Fig. 133

Fig. 134   Net patterns

Fig. 135. Net insertion

Net insertion (fig. 135). These diamonds make a very pretty grounding, either set separately or in a continuous pattern. The design is slight, although when it is worked in coarse cotton the effect is exceedingly handsome, especially if the inside, in addition to the star here given, be enriched with ordinary darning stitches worked in fine gold thread.

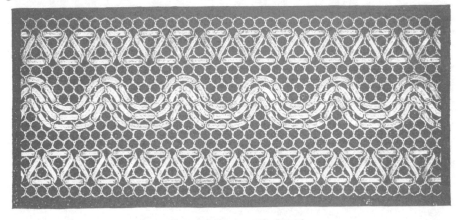

Fig. 136. Net tracery with braids

Net tracery with braids (fig. 136). In order to bring out the pattern and the colours, use a thicker thread such as pearl cotton. The little border can be used in conjunction with any of the preceding patterns, but care must be taken not to let it get twisted in the working. To prevent this, slip a coarse needle under the last stitch, and draw the braid flat over it.

Broad net lace tracery (fig. 137). The pattern of this pretty lace must first be transferred to stout paper. All the leaves and stalks, and the button-holing round the open centres of the flowers could be worked in a pale green, the two bottom flowers in Turkey red, the star-shaped one in blue, the calyx in which the stalks unite in dark red, and the little bells in the lightest green.

Fig. 137. Broad net lace tracery

Net darning. We conclude with some directions for darning net, a valuable art by means of which many a curious piece of old needlework is preserved. Coarse and fine net are all darned in the same way.

Laying the first thread (fig. 138). Tack the net which is to be darned, close to the defective part, upon coloured paper and cut the edges straight to the thread. Your thread must be of exactly the same size as that of which the net is made. It takes three rows of stitches to imitate the net ground; in the first place, as shown in fig. 138, cross-threads

61

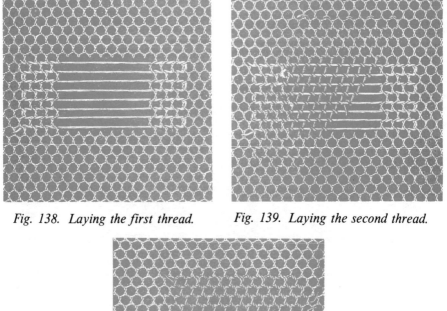

Fig. 138. Laying the first thread.   Fig. 139. Laying the second thread.

Fig. 140. Laying the third thread.

must be laid from side to side, carried as in darning, a little beyond the edges of the hole and so as to surround each mesh with a slanting stitch.

Laying the second thread (fig. 139). Secondly, beginning from one corner, threads are laid diagonally across the first layer. The cross-threads of the foundation are encircled by a stitch, made from right to left, the needle is then carried under the next horizontal bar, and the first layer of threads is overcast with similar stitches.

Laying the third thread (fig. 140). Thirdly, threads are carried across the second and first layers. They must start far enough from the edge for the second layer of threads to be overcast at the same time, so that there may be no loose threads left on the wrong side. In this third journey every diagonal thread of the foundation is to be encircled with a stitch taken upwards from below, the cut edges being strengthened in the same way. Then, to form the little cross in the fabric, the thread must be conducted by means of a second stitch under the single horizontal thread, outwards to the next diagonal thread.

In places where the net is worn it can be strengthened in the same manner, the stitches being made the way of the stuff.

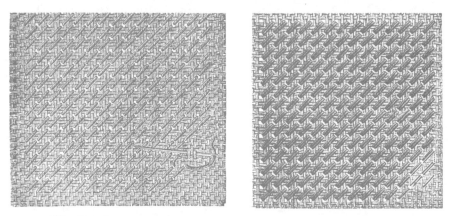

Fig. 141. First pattern   Fig. 142. Second pattern

Damask stitches. As a rule the pattern is simply outlined with stem and cord stitch, and the inside spaces are left plain. In spite of the time this simple tracing takes to do the effect is rather poor and scanty. If, however, the inside of the leaves and flowers be filled in with damask stitch, the result is very handsome.

Not only can the following stitches, which are suitable for any linen coarse or fine, be used for this kind of embroidery, but most of the net and lace patterns too, and these combined with button-holing and flat stitch produce charming effects. This kind of embroidery is generally done with a very coarse needle, to press the threads of the stuff closely together and make the light spaces between, which appear in many of the following illustrations.

First pattern (fig. 141). Carry the needle in a slanting direction over three threads and bring it out, from right to left, under three perpendicular ones, then, again slanting, over three threads, from left to right, and out again underneath three horizontal ones, downwards from above. Thus the first stitch lies across, from right to left, the second, lengthways. On the wrong side, the stitch forms a regular succession of steps.

Second pattern (fig. 142). This is worked exactly in the same manner as

63

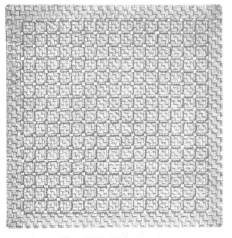

Fig. 143. Third pattern

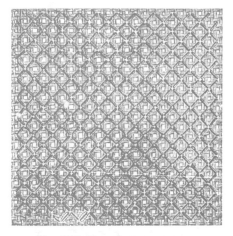

Fig. 144. Fourth pattern

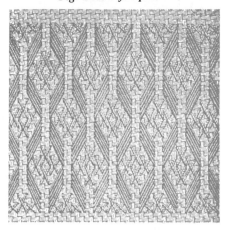

Fig. 145. Fifth pattern

Fig. 146. Sixth pattern

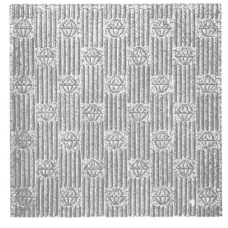

Fig. 147. Seventh pattern

Fig. 148. Eighth pattern

fig. 141 only that the second row of stitches touches the first so that two threads enter and issue from the same hole.

Third pattern (fig. 143). Though at first sight this stitch is very like the Holbein or stroke stitch, it is very different in the execution. It is worked in two rows, to and fro; in the first, you make all the vertical stitches side by side in the width of the stuff, drawing your thread very tightly; in the second, coming back, you make the horizontal stitches in a straight line, at right angles to the first stitches. On the wrong side the stitches are crossed; in thin stuffs, they show through, and quite alter the appearance of the right side.

Fourth pattern (fig. 144). In the first row, the thread is carried slanting upwards from right to left, over two threads, then downwards under two. Coming back, the stitches must be set the opposite way so that four threads meet in one hole.

Fifth pattern (fig. 145). This is worked like fig. 144, only that the stitches must cover three threads each way. In the second row, you take up one thread on the right and two on the left to form your stitches.

Sixth pattern (fig. 146). Here, the stitches form a chess-board pattern. You begin with a diagonal stitch over two threads and bring your needle up again into the same line it started from. The second stitch covers three threads, the third six, the fourth eight; the next three decrease successively in length in the same proportion.

Seventh pattern (fig. 147). Two kinds of cotton have to be used for this pattern, one of them soft and flat, like a soft cotton for the flat stitches, and the other strongly twisted like a pearl cotton for the cross stitches.

The five flat stitches cover three threads in width and six in height and lie from right to left and from left to right. In the second row, which must be two threads distant from the first, the stitches must lie in the contrary direction. In the lozenge-shaped space between make four cross-stitches over four threads in height and two in width.

Eighth pattern (figs. 148 and 149). Make five stitches over 8 horizontal threads, miss 6 threads and make another 5 stitches. The groups of long stitches above and beneath the first row encroach over two threads of the first group so that a space of only four threads remains between two groups. The stitch between these groups is generally known as the rococo stitch.

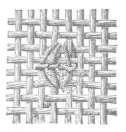

Fig. 149. Explanation of the Rococo stitch in fig. 148

Bring out your needle between the third and fourth of these threads and insert it again above, drawing it out afterwards between the second and third horizontal thread and securing the first stitch with a back-stitch. Make the three remaining stitches, as explained in fig. 149.

Ninth pattern (fig. 150). This consists of straight bands of diagonal flat stitches covering three threads each way, with spaces 8 threads wide between, ornamented with a small pattern in stroke stitch (see chapter on canvaswork and linen embroidery).

Damask stitch for figs. 102 and 104 (fig. 151). The stitches, here represented on a large scale, form the border to the square in cut open-work in fig. 104. The long diagonal stitches on either side can be made to look fuller and more distinct by using a soft, coarse cotton.

Tenth and eleventh patterns (figs. 152 and 153). The former of these is used for filling in the short stripe in fig. 104, the second for the long inside one. Fig. 152 is clear enough to need no explanation. With reference to fig. 153 it is, however, as well to point out that the shortest

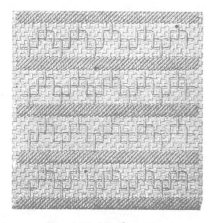

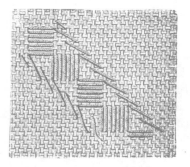

Fig. 151. Damask stitch for figs. 102 and 104

Fig. 150. Ninth pattern

stitch should cover 4 threads and the longest 12 (the rest is easily learnt from the illustration). This is a very suitable design for the decoration of large surfaces and combines well with any running diagonal pattern, when it can be made to form a large star which can be worked as a separate figure.

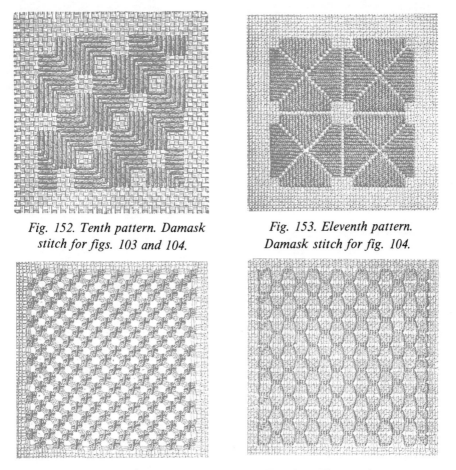

Fig. 152. Tenth pattern. Damask
stitch for figs. 103 and 104.

Fig. 153. Eleventh pattern.
Damask stitch for fig. 104.

Fig. 154. Twelfth pattern

Fig. 155. Thirteenth pattern

Twelfth pattern (fig. 154). In cases where this and the following stitches are to be executed on a light, transparent stuff, it is best to use a very strongly twisted thread, such as fine pearl cotton, instead of a softer and looser material. A stiff thread compresses the threads of the stuff better and the open spaces thus made in it are rendered more visible.

Count 6 threads vertically, put in the needle and draw it through from right to left, underneath 3 diagonal threads. For the next stitch,

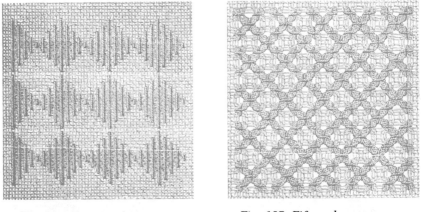

Fig. 156. Fourteenth pattern   *Fig. 157. Fifteenth pattern*

carry it upwards over 6 threads, and back under 3. The second row is worked back over the first in the same way. Leave 6 threads between each row.

Thirteenth pattern (fig. 155). Carry the thread from right to left over four vertical threads and under the same number of horizontal ones. The second row of stitches touches the first so that the thread it is worked with seems to be drawn through under the same threads of the stuff as the one the first row was worked with.

Fourteenth pattern (fig. 156). Here the stitches, contrary to those in fig. 146, are set vertically. The first stitch covers 2 threads, the second 6, the third 10, the fourth 14, the fifth 18. The longest stitches of two checks always meet in the same hole.

Fifteenth pattern (fig. 157). Cover the whole expanse with rows of stitches such as are described in fig. 154, with intervals of 12 threads between them.
    These rows are intersected by others, to which the thread is passed from between the sixth and seventh of the 12 threads between the first rows. Where the stitches of the two rows meet, the working thread of the second row must be drawn through, under that of the first.

Sixteenth pattern (fig. 158). Between every two rows of cross-stitch leave an interval of 6 threads, counting those on each side of the rows. Over these 6 threads work 2 rows as shown in fig. 142 but so that in the second the lower stitch of the first row and the upper one of the second cover the same threads.

Fig. 158. Sixteenth pattern

Fig. 159. Seventeenth pattern

Seventeenth pattern (fig. 159). This consists of stripes, 4 stitches wide like those of fig. 154, with 3 threads between, which are overcast in the ordinary manner.

Eighteenth pattern (fig. 160). Small squares of 7 stitches, inclined alternately to the right and left, and so formed that the longest stitch of one square is crossed by the first short stitch of the next so that a space only 6 threads wide and 4 long remains uncovered. The intervening stripes are filled with 3 rows of overcasting stitches covering 2 threads each way.

Nineteenth pattern (fig. 161). The steps formed by this pattern are 11 stitches high and 11 wide and each stitch covers 4 threads.

Eight threads intervene between each row of steps, which are

Fig. 160. Eighteenth pattern

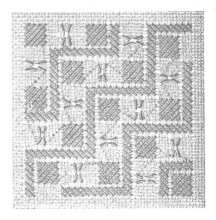

Fig. 161. Nineteenth pattern

69

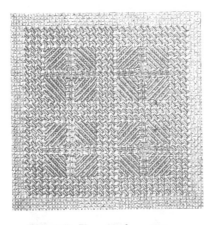

Fig. 162. Twentieth pattern

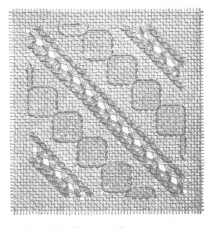

Fig. 163. Twenty-first pattern

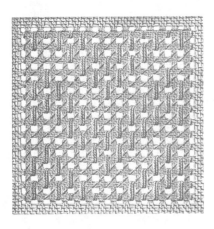

Fig. 164. Twenty-second pattern

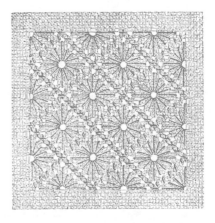

Fig. 165. Twenty-third pattern

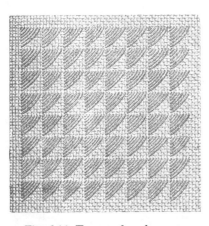

Fig. 166. Twenty-fourth pattern

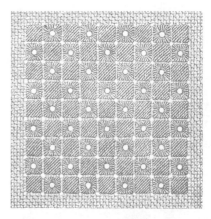

Fig. 167. Twenty-fifth pattern

covered at the bend by a square of stitches, from the last of which the thread is carried on at once to the four single stitches.

Twentieth pattern (fig. 162). The 4 squares set opposite to each other, with 2 threads between, are edged all round by 3 rows of overcasting.

Twenty-first pattern (fig. 163). Begin by rows of stitches like those described in fig. 154, over 4 and 2 threads, with 4 threads between, not counting those covered with cross-stitch. Between the two rows of cross-stitch, join 6 threads together by a back-stitch and carry your thread over the two last of the 6 to the 2 first of the next cluster. The narrow diagonal stripes are separated by 24 threads, exclusive of those covered by the cross-stitches. These spaces are filled in with squares 10 threads wide and 10 long formed by back-stitches crossed on the wrong side.

Twenty-second pattern (fig. 164). In the closer stuffs of a coarse texture, the threads of which do not admit of being drawn together as you can those of a loose thin stuff, where by simply pulling your thread a little tighter you get open spaces, you must begin by cutting out every fourth or fifth thread. After, you overcast all the rows, first one way and then the other with stitches covering 4 threads each way. On this foundation use a strong, loosely twisted cotton such as Coton à broder to make long stitches as indicated in the illustration.

Twenty-third pattern (fig. 165). From the point where the thread comes out of the stuff, make 16 stitches, all coming out of the same hole and over 8, 6, 4 and 6 threads, thus forming a star. Leave an interval of four threads between the stars, and unite the intervening threads by cross-stitches one way and whip-stitches the other.

Twenty-fourth pattern (fig. 166). Make a succession of diagonal stitches, increasing in length and advancing one thread at a time until the seventh stitch covers seven threads, and completes the triangle. Then begin a second triangle on the nearest, adjacent thread.

Twenty-fifth pattern (fig. 167). Cover your whole surface with squares of 11 stitches and fill in the intervening squares with 24 stitches, all radiating from one centre.

Twenty-sixth pattern (fig. 168). Diagonal trellised stripes, made as indicated in fig. 164 and overcast, form the ground. Twelve threads are to be left between the stripes, upon which work six-cornered, lozenge-shaped groups of stitches, set at right angles to each other, in diagonal rows.

Fig. 168. Twenty-sixth pattern

Twenty-seventh pattern (fig. 169). We conclude our chapter with a circular design which combines a variety of stitches. It also introduces our workers to two new patterns as well as to an advantageous way of hiding the junction of several kinds of stitches by semicircles of button-hole stitching.

Fig. 169. Twenty-seventh pattern

Strip in flat and raised satin stitch, and Madeira embroidery.

White Embroidery

We have retained the familiar term, white embroidery, for this kind of needlework for convenience sake in spite of its inaccuracy now that coloured materials are quite as much used for it as white.

Many kinds of whitework are best worked with a frame or hoop (see chapter on Useful Information).

Tracing patterns. Patterns are often to be had ready traced but as it is often necessary to repeat, enlarge, or reduce them descriptions of several modes of doing so will be found at the end of the penultimate chapter.

Materials. A loose, soft make of cotton, the looser the better and very little twisted, is the best material for whitework embroidery. We recommend Coton à broder or stranded cotton.

Outlining and padding. The outlining of a pattern is a very important preliminary. A want of precision in the ultimate effect is often due merely to careless outlining. This part of the work should be done with rather a coarser cotton than the embroidery itself. Fasten in the thread by a few running stitches, never with a knot, a rule to be observed also in embroidering except in very rare cases. Finish off your thread by drawing it through the tracing stitches, or through some part of the pattern that is already finished. Fill in the spaces between the lines with a padding of run threads, run loosely so that they lie thickly and solidly in the centre and shade off on both sides. The fullness and roundness of embroidery depends on the firmness of this sub-stratum of threads. The outlining and the padding of the different rounded and pointed scallops, as well as of other figures that occur in white embroidery, are illustrated in figs. 180, 181, 182, 183, 184, 186, 188, 189 and 190.

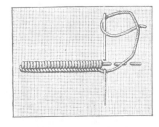

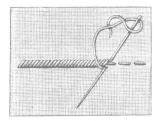

Fig. 170. Blanket, or button-hole stitch.   *Fig. 171. Straight stem stitch*

Blanket, or button-hole stitch (fig. 170). Work from left to right; run in a foundation line, hold down the working thread below the run line with the right thumb; insert the needle above and bring it out below the run line but above the working thread; tighten the loop thus formed without drawing up the stuff, and continue in this manner, setting your stitches closely and regularly, side by side.

Straight stem stitch (fig. 171). Work from left to right. The needle must always be inserted above the run thread and brought out underneath it. In the case of a very delicate pattern take up only just as much stuff as the run thread covers.

Sloping stem stitch (fig. 172). Work without a run thread; insert the needle from right to left in a slanting direction, under 1 or 2 horizontal threads and 5 or 6 perpendicular ones so that each stitch reaches half-way back to the last.

   This kind of stem stitch is chiefly used for the fine up-strokes of letters and numbers and for linen embroidery.

Back-stitching (fig. 173). Back-stitching, that is small, even stitches set closely together, is done from right to left along a straight line and is chiefly used for filling in the centres of letters, leaves and flowers.

Crossed back-stitch (figs. 174 and 175). Used, generally speaking, only for very transparent materials as a 'shadow' design; it forms a close seam of cross-stitch on the wrong side and two straight rows of back-stitching on the right. To work, insert the needle as if for an ordinary

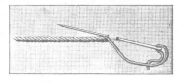

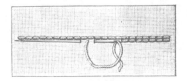

Fig. 172. Sloping stem stitch   *Fig. 173. Back-stitching*

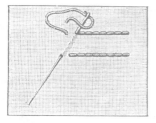

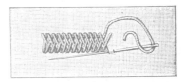

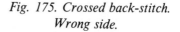

*Fig. 175. Crossed back-stitch.
Wrong side.*

Fig. 174. Crossed back-stitch. Right side.

back-stitch, pass it under the stuff, sloping it a little towards the second outline of the pattern, and draw it out almost in front of the first stitch. After making a back-stitch, pass the needle up again under the stuff and bring it out at the spot where the next stitch is to be.

Fig. 175 shows the interlacing of the stitches on the wrong side, and the way in which this stitch, when it is used for filling in centres, can be worked on the right side.

Simple knot stitch (fig. 176). This consists of two back-stitches, side by side, covering the same threads; it is chiefly used for filling in leaves, or in conjunction with flat stitch.

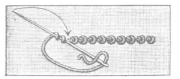

Fig. 176. Simple knot stitch

Fig. 177. Twisted knot stitch

Twisted knot stitch (French knot) (fig. 177). To work hold the working thread down with the thumb close to the spot where you first brought it out, twist it consistently once, twice or thrice round the needle, turn the needle round from left to right, following the direction indicated by the arrow, pass it through the fabric at the place which is marked by a dot, and draw it out at the place where the next stitch is to be.

Post stitch (Bullion knot) (fig. 178). Something like knot stitch and much used for patterns composed of small flowers and leaves, where it often takes the place of raised satin stitch. The illustration represents five leaves finished and the sixth in process of being worked.

To work, bring the needle up from the back and twist the thread round it as many times as the length of the stitch requires, hold the left thumb on the species of curl thus formed, and passing the needle and thread through it, insert it at the end of the leaf where it first came out, and draw it out at the right place for the next stitch.

75

Button-hole bars (fig. 179). When a pattern is ornamented with open-work bars, begin by tracing the outside parallel lines. Then button-hole the whole lower line and the upper one till you come to the place where the first bar is to be; then you carry your thread across and bring up the needle from below through one of the loops, as shown in the figure. Lay three threads in this manner, inserting your needle the third time one loop further on, then cover the three threads thickly with button-holing.

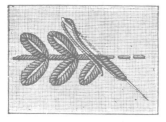

Fig. 178. Post stitch   Fig. 179. Button-hole bars

Different kinds of scallops (figs. 180, 181, 182). The outlining, padding and button-holing of these scallops is executed in the manner already described. Be careful to adapt the length of the stitches to the shape and size of the scallops. If they are pointed (figs. 181, 182), the stitches will have to be set very closely together on the inner line and a little play allowed them on the outer to come exactly to the point, which should be very sharply defined.

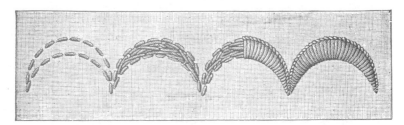

Fig. 180. Semi-circular, button-holed scallops.

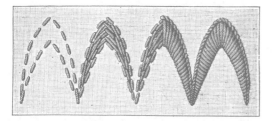

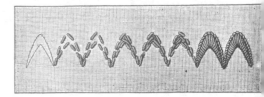

Fig. 181. Large, pointed, button-holed scallops.   Fig. 182. Small, pointed, button-holed scallops

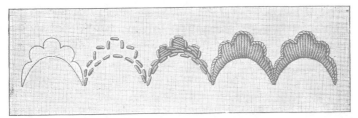

Fig. 183. Rounded rose scallops

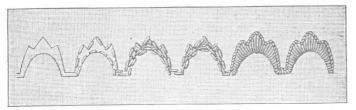

Fig. 184. Pointed rose scallops

Rose scallops (figs. 183 and 184). These are large button-holed scallops with indented edges, in the one case rounded at the top and sharply pointed at the join, in the other pointed at the top and joined at the bottom by a straight bar of button-holing.

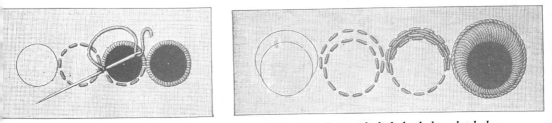

Fig. 185. Overcast eyelet holes   *Fig. 186. Button-holed shaded eyelet holes*

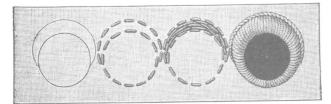

Fig. 187. Shaded eyelet holes half overcast, half button-holed.

Eyelet holes (figs. 185, 186, 187). Outline the eyelet holes very carefully first by running a thread round them, then cut out the enclosed stuff with a sharp pair of finely pointed scissors or a stiletto, and edge the hole with plain overcasting stitches, worked from left to right.

When you have a long row of eyelet holes to make, outline the upper and lower halves alternately, first on one side and then on the other, using two threads, and then overcast them in the same way. The double crossing of the working threads between the eyelet holes makes them much stronger than if each hole were finished off separately, the thread passed underneath from one to the other.

The lower halves of shaded eyelet holes (see figs. 186 and 187) are worked with very short stitches and the upper halves with long ones; they may be edged entirely, either with button-holing or overcasting, or half with one and half with the other.

Six leaves in raised satin stitch (fig. 188). Raised satin stitch is chiefly used for working flowers, leaves, petals, dots, initials and monograms. After tracing the outline of the design, fill in the centres with a padding of long, close stitches and then, beginning always at the point of the leaf, cover it with flat, perfectly even stitches, worked from right to left, as in illustration A. B illustrates a leaf divided through the middle by a line of overcasting; C, one with a corded vein; D, a divided leaf worked in sloping satin stitch; E, a leaf with a corded vein and framed in sloping satin stitch; F, a leaf worked half in satin stitch, half in back-stitch and straight stem stitch.

Leaves and flowers of all descriptions can be executed in any of these stitches, and in different combinations of the same.

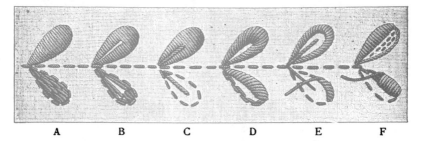

A   B   C   D   E   F

Fig. 188. Six leaves in raised satin stitch

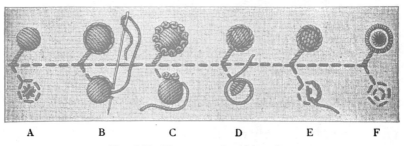

A   B   C   D   E   F

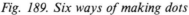

Fig. 189. Six ways of making dots

Fig. 190. Venetian embroidery

Six ways of making dots (fig. 189). Dots, when they are well made, are exceedingly effective in white embroidery, particularly if they are worked in a variety of stitches. Dot A is worked in raised satin stitch; B, in raised satin stitch, framed in back-stitch; C, in raised satin stitch, framed in twisted knot stitch; D is composed of several post stitches of different lengths, set in a frame of stem stitches; E is worked in back-stitch, and F has as centre a small eyelet hole with a corded setting.

Venetian embroidery (fig. 190). Scallops worked in very high relief are called Venetian embroidery, an imitation on stuff of Venetian lace.

Real Venetian point is entirely needle-made; in the embroidered imitations of it the stuff takes the place of the needle-made lace foundation. To make it more like the original, however, the ground is seldom left plain, but is covered with fancy stitches, such as are represented in the illustration. The button-hole bars may be made with or without picots. A full description of the latter will be found in the chapters on net embroidery and Irish lace (see Volume 3 in this series). The space to be button-holed must be well padded, for thereon depends the roundness of the embroidery. For this purpose take at least 6 thicknesses of thread and fasten them down on to the pattern with loose stitches, laying on extra threads and cutting them gradually away according to the width the line is to be. The stuff underneath the button-hole bars should only be cut away when the embroidery is quite finished.

Fig. 191. Renaissance embroidery

Renaissance embroidery (figs. 191 and 192). This is the term applied, more especially in France, to embroidery patterns which are worked entirely in button-holing and connected by interior button-hole bars without picots, as shown in the two accompanying figures. (The outside edge in fig. 192 is embellished with picots.)

Fig. 192. Renaissance embroidery

Richelieu embroidery (fig. 193). The name given to embroidery of a similar kind to Renaissance in which the connecting bars, instead of being left plain as they are in the Renaissance embroidery, are ornamented with picots.

Fig. 193. Richelieu embroidery

Madeira work (figs. 194, 195, 196). This kind of embroidery consists chiefly of eyelet holes and is distinguished for the excellence of its workmanship. It used to be known as English but is now generally called Madeira work, from the island where it originated. The scallops in figs. 194 and 196 are bordered with shaded eyelet holes, worked half in button-hole stitch, half in overcasting; the finely scalloped edge in fig. 195 is entirely button-holed. In working eyelet holes the material must always be turned in, up to the inside line, and completely worked in underneath the stitches, in order that no loose threads may be visible on the wrong side.

Alphabets for monograms (figs. 197 to 202). On account of the difficulty of devising a good monogram for marking under-linen, we show here two alphabets by the aid of which our workers will be able to compose their own.

The letters are of a good medium size which can be magnified or reduced according to the worker's own taste.

For any such modifications, we would again draw our reader's attention to the directions given in the penultimate chapter. The first three plates represent large wide letters intended to contain or encompass the more elongated ones represented in the fourth and fifth plates, figs. 200 and 201.

The interlacing of the letters requires to be carefully done, and our workers should study the following specimens so as to learn the stitches which are most suitable for this branch of embroidery.

Figs. 194–196. Madeira work

Fig. 197. Alphabets for monograms. Outside letters A to H.

Fig. 198. Alphabets for monograms. Outside letters J to Q.

Fig. 199. Alphabets for monograms. Outside letters R to Y.

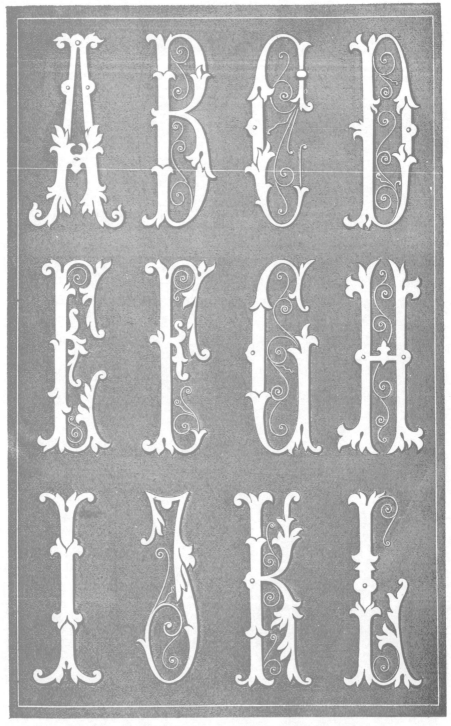

Fig. 200. Alphabets for monograms. Inside letters A to L.

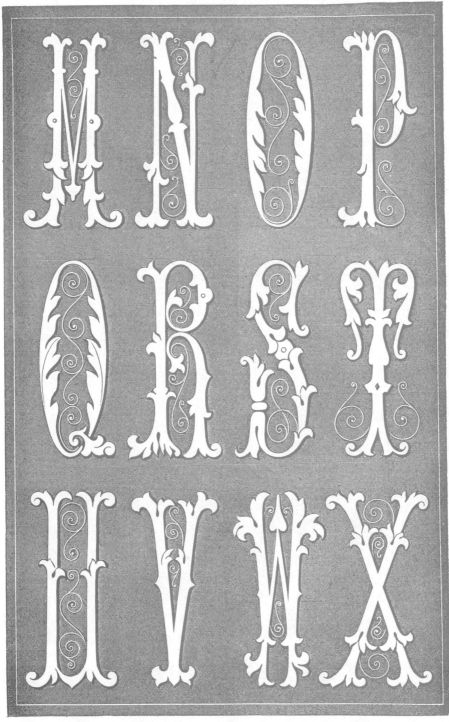

Fig. 201. Alphabets for monograms. Inside letters M to X.

Fig. 203. Monogram composed
of letters A and D

Fig. 204. Monogram composed
of letters V and S

drawn from the alphabets of monograms

Monogram composed of letters A and D (fig. 203). Here, letter A is worked in flat satin stitch and set in stem stitch. D, as a contrast to A, is embroidered in transverse bars. The little ornaments may be worked according to fancy, either in white or in colours.

Monogram composed of letters V and S (fig. 204). The flat satin stitch in both letters is worked in white; the setting is in short stem stitch in red, for example, or if preferred, in knotted back-stitch.

Monogram composed of letters R and C (fig. 205). These are worked in black and grey, for mourning; the way C is divided admits of a variety in the stitch: the back-stitches in the illustration, for instance, may be replaced by very small eyelet holes.

Fig. 202. Alphabets for monograms. Last inside and outside letters.

*Fig. 205. Monogram composed
of letters R and C*

*Fig. 206. Monogram composed
of letters G and E*

drawn from the alphabets of monograms

Monogram composed of letters G and E (fig. 206). The flat satin stitching and back-stitching in E, and the stem-stitched edges of G are worked in white Coton à broder DMC; the inside of G in ivory white stranded cotton.

Border (fig. 207). The original of fig. 207 was in blue and red, indigo blue for the grounding and cardinal red for the setting in stem-stitch. The herring-boning along the edges of the pattern, top and bottom, is also in red.

Should a different selection of colours be made it is important to remember that in all cases a sharp contrast is desirable.

Alphabet and numerals left blank and outlined by the grounding, worked in satin stitch (figs. 208 to 212). The border worked in satin stitch, illustrated in fig. 207, suggested to us the idea of an alphabet and numerals to be left blank and outlined by a grounding in satin stitch.

*Fig. 207. Border in padded satin stitch, stem stitch and herring-bone using colours such
as indigo blue 311 and Cardinal red 606.*

89

Fig. 208. Alphabet left blank and outlined by the grounding. Letters A to N.

Our limited space prevents us from giving all the letters in the diagonal position they are intended to occupy on the article itself: only O and W are represented in the right position. No difficulty will be found in copying the other letters to give them the proper direction.

In order to economize room, J and H are represented in one square but they are easily distinguishable from each other.

Fig. 210 represents the numerals executed in the same way. We should like to draw our reader's attention to a few other ways in which

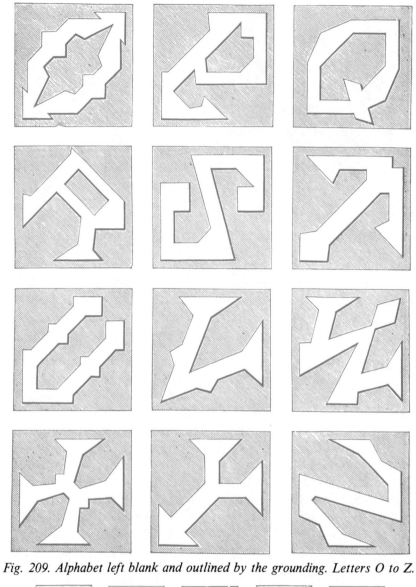

Fig. 209. Alphabet left blank and outlined by the grounding. Letters O to Z.

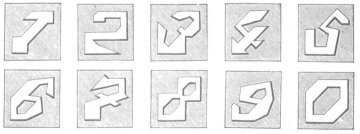

Fig. 210. Numerals left blank and outlined by the grounding

Fig. 211. Letter O, from the
alphabet given in figs. 208 and 209.

Fig. 212. Letter W, from the
alphabet given in figs. 208 and 209.

letters and numerals may be outlined by the background; the solid
parts can be worked, for example, either in plain or twisted knot stitch
(figs. 176 and 177); in very fine chain stitch; in old German knot or
bead stitch (fig. 375), or even in piqué embroidery (fig. 381).

Border, outlined by grounding, worked in satin and stem stitch (fig. 213).
The grounding of this pattern is worked on stiff white linen, say,
entirely in Turkish red and the outlining in black. The same pattern
can equally well be worked on gauzes and other transparent stuffs but
with 2 or 3 strands of stranded cotton instead of Coton à broder
DMC, for the solid parts. Two different values of the same colour, one
dark and one very light, may be preferred, employing always the
lighter shade for the grounding and the darker for the setting.

Be careful, in the grounding, not to make the red stitches near the
edge longer than they are represented in the illustration and to set the
black stem stitches as close as possible to the grounding.

Flower garland in different kinds of stitches (figs. 214 and 215). Most of
the stitches described at the beginning of this chapter will be found in
this graceful garland, in the execution of which a considerable variety
of colours can be introduced. The rose-buds may be worked, for
example, in two shades of pistachio green and of geranium, in the
stitches described in figs. 172, 176, 188 A; the forget-me-nots, in two
or even three shades of indigo blue, in raised satin stitch and knotted

*Opposite: Fig. 213 (left). Border, outlined by the grounding worked in satin and
stem stitch. Colours: Turkish red 321 and black 310. Fig. 214 (right). Flower garland in
different kinds of stitches. Colours: Geranium 353 and 351, indigo blue 311 and 334,
pistachio 966 and 943, mahogany 838 and lemon 445.*

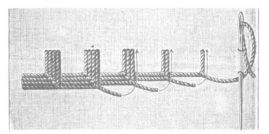

Fig. 215. Showing the working of the outside stitches in fig. 214.

stitch; the slender green leaves in grey-green, or lime-green, the stamens in lemon yellow, and the stalks of the roses in mahogany brown.

The border that completes this charming pattern consists of four rows of button-holing worked in four colours. The first row in our illustration is worked in pale pink, followed by three shades of green, the palest of which is used for the second row of stitches.

When these rows are worked upon a satin or cambric foundation it is advisable to begin by making a small drawing in which the height of the stitches and the distance between them are accurately marked out, then prick the pattern through and pounce it upon the material beneath. When they are worked on a material the threads of which can be counted no such precaution is necessary.

Insertion in satin and stem stitch (fig. 216). Owing to the shortness of the stitches, this pattern is easier to work than the foregoing ones. The

Fig. 216. Insertion in satin and stem stitch. Colours: Cardinal red 606, geranium 353, lime 704 and 699, or indigo 311 and 334 with moss green 469 and 471, or purple 553 and rust 301 and 300.

94

little flowers are embroidered alternately in dark and light red, the light red flowers being set in dark red surrounds and vice versa. The interior of the leaves is in light green and the setting, as well as the connecting bars, in dark green.

Stripes of embroidery with lace insertion between (fig. 217). We conclude this chapter by showing how stripes of embroidery can be used alone, or in conjunction, either with bands of open-work, or lace, crochet, or net insertion. Such combinations are useful for ornamenting aprons, table-cloths, curtains, etc., every description in short of household linen and of children's garments.

Fig. 217. Stripes of embroidery with insertion between

Stripe of gold embroidery in gold thread, purl, and flattened gold wire.

Flat Stitch & Gold Embroidery

The terms flat stitch (forms of satin stitch) and gold embroidery suggest as a rule needlework upon rich materials such as velvet, brocade, plush and the like.

Nevertheless, a great deal of beautiful embroidery is to be found in silk and gold thread upon quite common stuffs; Persian and Moorish embroidery, for instance, both remarkable for their delicacy and minuteness, are executed upon ordinary linen, or cotton fabrics.

As a fact, the material is quite a secondary matter; almost any will do equally well as a foundation for the stitches described in these pages. Flat satin stitch, and some of the other stitches used in gold embroidery, can be worked with any kind of thread, but best of all with the DMC cottons.

Flat stitch embroidery. Decorative designs, and conventional flowers, are the most suitable for flat stitch embroidery; a faithful represent-ation of natural flowers should not be attempted unless it be so well executed as to produce the effect of a painting and thus possess real artistic merit.

Encroaching flat stitch (fig. 218). Small delicate flowers, leaves, and arabesques should in preference be worked either in straight flat stitch (figs. 188 and 189) or in encroaching flat stitch. The stitches should all be of equal length, the length to be determined by the quality of the thread, a fine thread necessitating short, and a coarse one long, stitches. The stitches should run one into the other, as shown in the

96

illustration. They are worked in rows, those of the second row encroaching on those of the first and fitting into one another.

Work your flowers and leaves from the point, never from the calyx or stalk. If they are to be shaded, begin by choosing the right shade for the outside edge, varying the depth according to the light in which the object is to be placed. The stitches should always follow the direction of the drawing.

Fig. 218. Encroaching flat stitch

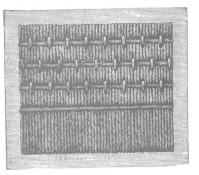

Fig. 219. Oriental stitch

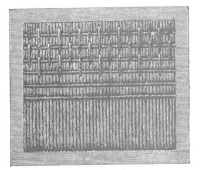

Fig. 220. Oriental stitch

Fig. 221. Oriental stitch

Oriental stitch (figs. 219, 220, 221). The three following stitches, which we have grouped under one heading, are known also under the name of Renaissance or Arabic stitches. We have used the term Oriental because they are to be met with in almost all Oriental needlework and probably derive their origin from Asia, whose inhabitants have at all times been renowned for the beauty of their embroideries.

These kinds of stitches are only suitable for large, bold designs. Draw in the vertical threads first; work with a soft, silky thread, ideally untwisted (say, several strands of stripped stranded cotton) so that each stitch can be close to its neighbours: you will always get a better effect if, rather than beginning a second stitch close to where the first ended, you take the thread back underneath the stuff and begin your next stitch in a line with the first so that all the stitches of the first layer, which form the grounding, are carried from the top to the bottom. The same directions apply to figs. 220, 221, 223.

When you have laid your vertical threads, stretch threads horizontally across and fasten them down with isolated stitches set six vertical threads apart. The position of these fastening stitches on the transverse threads must alternate in each row, as indicated in fig. 219.

For fig. 220, make a similar grounding to the one above described, laying the horizontal threads a little closer together and making the fastening stitches over two threads.

In fig. 221, the second threads are carried diagonally across the foundation-threads and the fastening stitches are given a similar direction.

For these stitches, use either one material only, a fleecy thread like soft cotton DMC for instance, or else two, such as soft cotton DMC for the grounding, and a material with a strong twist like pearl cotton DMC for the stem stitch.

Fig. 222. Plaited stitch   Fig. 223. Mosaic stitch

Plaited stitch (fig. 222). When the vertical stitches are laid, a kind of weave is formed in the following way. Using a blunt-edged needle, pass the thread three times alternately under and over three foundation threads. To do this very accurately, you must take the thread back, underneath, to its starting-point, and consequently always make your stitch from right to left.

If you have chosen a washing material, and DMC cottons to work with, use one colour of cotton for the foundation, and China white DMC for the plaited stitch.

Mosaic stitch (fig. 223). In old embroideries we often find this stitch, employed as a substitute for plush or other costly stuffs, appliquéd on to the foundation. It is executed in the same manner as the four preceding stitches but can only be done in thick twist, such as pearl cottons DMC.

Each stitch should be made separately, and must pass underneath the foundation, so that the threads which form the pattern are not flat, as they are in the preceding examples, but slightly rounded.

Fig. 224. Border in Persian stitch

Border in Persian stitch (fig. 224). This stitch, of Persian origin, resembles the one represented in fig. 174. Instead of bringing the needle out, however, as indicated in fig. 175, take it back as you see in the illustration to the space between the outlines of the drawing, and behind the thread that forms the next stitch. Before filling in the pattern, outline it with short stem stitches, or a fine cord, laid on and secured with invisible stitches.

This graceful design, which can be utilised in various ways, is formed of leaves of 7 lobes worked alternately in dark and light green, of flowers of 3 red petals and yellow centres, and of small leaves in violet. The setting, throughout, is worked either in black or in dark brown.

Stripe worked in encroaching flat and knot stitch (fig. 225). This pattern, simple as it is, will be found both useful and effective for the trimming of all kinds of articles of dress. The bottom edge should be finished off with rounded scallops or toothed vandykes worked in button-hole stitch. The encroaching satin stitch flowers are worked alternately in two shades of geranium red, and the leaves alternately in two shades of green; the centres of the flowers are worked in knot stitch, in old gold.

Bouquet in straight and encroaching flat stitch (fig. 226). As we have already observed, it is by no means easy to arrange the colours in an

Fig. 225. Stripe worked in encroaching flat and knot stitch. Colours: geranium 351 and 353 (flowers), rust 729 (knots), and 471 and 469 (foliage).

embroidery of this kind so as to obtain a really artistic effect. Whether the design be a conventional one or not, the great point is to put in the lights and shadows at the right place. If you want to make a faithful copy of a natural flower, take the flower itself, or a coloured botanical drawing of it, and if possible a good black and white drawing of the same, match the colours in 6 or 7 shades by the flower itself, keeping

Fig. 226. Bouquet in straight and encroaching flat stitch. Colours: indigo blue 311, 322, 334 (forget-me-nots), rust 729 and 832, purple 554, 553 and 550 and pistachio 966 (other flowers), green 472, 469, 935 and 580 (foliage) and 451 and 3023 (stalks).

them all rather paler in tone, and take the black and white drawing as a guide for the lights and shadows. The colours for the leaves and petals, which should always be worked from the outside, should be chosen with a view to their blending well together. The stamens and the centres of the flowers should be left to the last, but the veins and ribs of the leaves should always be put in before the grounding.

For embroideries of this kind, suitable materials must be selected; the more delicate and minute the design and the more varied the colouring, the softer and finer should be the quality of the material employed.

Fig. 227. Flowers embroidered in the Chinese manner

Flowers embroidered in the Chinese manner (fig. 227). All Chinese embroidery displays undoubted originality and wonderful skill and judgment in the choice of material and colour. It excels particularly in the representation of figures, flowers, and animals, but differs from European work in that instead of using flat stitch and making the colours blend together as we do, the Chinese put them side by side without intermediate tones, or they sometimes work the whole pattern in knot stitch. The little knots formed by this stitch are sometimes set in gold thread.

Often, too, instead of combining a number of colours as we do, the Chinese fill in the whole leaf with long stitches and upon this foundation draw the veins in a different stitch and colour. They embroider even the flowers in the same way, in very fine thread, filling in the whole ground first with stitches set very closely together and marking in the seed vessels afterwards with diminutive knots, wide apart.

Chinese encroaching flat stitch (fig. 228). Another easy kind of embroidery, common in China, is done in encroaching flat stitch. The branch represented in our drawing, taken from a large design, is

Fig. 228. Chinese encroaching flat stitch

executed in three shades of yellow, resembling those of the old gold series on the DMC colour card.

The stitches of the different rows encroach upon one another, as the working detail shows, and the three shades alternate in regular succession. Flowers, butterflies and birds are represented in Chinese embroidery executed in this manner. It is a style that is adapted to stuffs of all kinds, washing materials as well as others, and can be worked in the hand and with any of the DMC threads and cottons.

Raised embroidery (figs. 229 and 230). Raised embroidery worked in colours must be stuffed or padded first like the white embroidery in fig. 190. If you outline your design with a cord, secure it on the right side with invisible stitches, untwisting the cord slightly as you insert your needle and thread so that the stitch may be hidden between the strands. Use a soft cotton, or another length of suitable padding thread for the padding. These cottons are to be had in all the colours indicated in the DMC colour card, and are the most suitable for the kind of work.

If you work close lines of satin stitch in silk or cotton on top of a 'padding' of Coton à broder you will produce an effect which will bear

Raised embroidery

Fig. 229. Preparatory work   *Fig. 230. Work completed.*

more resemblance to appliqué work than to embroidery. The centres of the flowers are filled in with knot stitches which are either set directly on the stuff or on an embroidered ground.

Embroidery in the Turkish style (figs. 231 and 232). This again is a style of embroidery different from any we are accustomed to. The solid raised parts are first padded with common coarse cotton and then worked over with gold, silver or silk thread.

Contrary to what is noticeable in the real Turkish embroidery, the preparatory work here is very carefully done, with several threads of, say, pearl cotton DMC used as one. A rope of five threads is laid down, and carried from right to left and from left to right across the width of the pattern. After laying it across to the right, as explained in fig. 230, bring the needle out a little beyond the space occupied by the threads, insert it behind them and passing it under the stuff draw it out at the spot indicated by the arrow. The stitch that secures the threads should be sufficiently long to give them a little play so that they may

Embroidery in the Turkish style

Fig. 231. Preparatory work   *Fig. 232. Work completed*

lie perfectly parallel, side by side, over the whole width of the pattern.

This kind of work can be done on woollen or cotton materials, and generally speaking, with DMC cottons, and gold thread shot with colour (DMC).

Very pretty effects can be obtained by a combination of three values of Cardinal red, with Chinese white, gold and dark blue or with Chinese white, gold and light blue.

This kind of embroidery may be regarded as the transition from satin stitch to gold embroidery.

Gold embroidery. Until recently, and from the end of the eighteenth century, gold embroidery has been almost exclusively confined to those who made it a profession; amateurs have seldom attempted what – it was commonly supposed – required an apprenticeship of nine years to attain any proficiency in. But now the art of gold embroidery has revived and is being taken up and practised with success even by those to whom needlework is nothing more than an agreeable recreation.

Implements and materials. The first and needful requisites for gold embroidery are a strong frame, a spindle, two pressers, one flat and the other convex, a curved knife, a pricker or stiletto, and a tray to contain the materials.

Fig. 233. Embroidery frame for gold embroidery

Embroidery frame (fig. 233). The frame represented here is only suitable for small pieces of embroidery; for larger ones, which have to be done piece by piece, round bars on which to roll up the stuff are desirable as sharp wooden edges are so apt to mark the stuff.

Every gold embroidery, on whatever material it may be executed, requires a stout foundation which has to be sewn into the frame: hold the webbing loosely, almost in folds, and stretch the stuff very tightly. Sew on a stout cord to the edges of the foundation which are nearest the stretchers, setting the stitches 3 or 4 cm. apart, then put the frame together and stretch the material laterally to its fullest extent by passing a piece of string in and out through the cord at the edge and over the stretchers. Draw up the bracing until the foundation is strained evenly and tightly. Upon this firm foundation lay the stuff which you are going to embroider and hem or herring-bone it down, taking care to keep it perfectly even with the thread of the foundation and, if possible, more tightly stretched, to prevent it from being wrinkled or puckered when you come to take it off the backing.

Fig. 234. The spindle

The spindle (fig. 234). The spindle to wind the gold thread upon should be 20 cm. long and made of hard wood. Cover the round stalk and part of the prongs with a double thread of pale yellow Coton à broder and finish off with a loop to which you fasten the gold thread that you wind round the stalk.

The pressers (figs. 235 and 236). These so called 'pressers' are small rectangular boards with a handle in the middle. The convex one, fig. 235, should be 15 cm. long by 9 broad; the other, fig. 236, which is quite flat, should be 32 cm. by 20.

Having cut out your pattern in cartridge paper, lay it down upon a board thinly spread with embroidery paste, let it get thoroughly impregnated with the paste and then transfer it carefully to its proper

Fig. 235. Convex presser, for pressing the stuff on the wrong side.

Fig. 236. Flat presser for laying on the pattern

place on the stuff; press it closely down with the large presser, and with the little convex one rub the stuff firmly from beneath to make it adhere closely to the pasted pattern; small pointed leaves and flowers will be found to need sewing down, as you will observe in fig. 239, where each point is secured by stitches. The embroidery should not be begun until the paste is perfectly dry, and the pattern adheres firmly to the stuff.

The knife (fig. 237). Most gold embroideries require a foundation of stout cartridge paper and, in the case of very delicate designs, the paper should further be covered with kid, pasted upon it.

Transfer the design on to the paper or kid in the manner described in the concluding chapter, and cut it out with the knife. You can only make very short incisions with this tool, which should be kept extremely sharp and held with the point outwards and the rounded part towards you, as shown in the drawing.

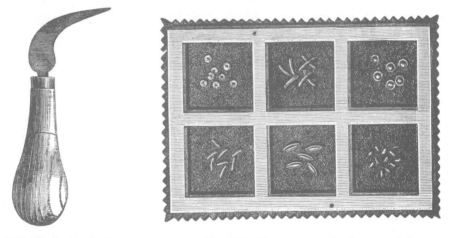

Fig. 237. The knife. Reduced scale.   *Fig. 238. Tray to contain the materials*

Tray to contain the materials (fig. 238). Cut out as many divisions in a thin board or sheet of stout cardboard as you will require materials for your embroidery; these include not only gold thread of all kinds but likewise beads and spangles of all sorts and sizes as well as bright and dead gold and silver purl, or bullion, as it is also called. For the pieces of purl alone, which should be cut ready to hand, you should have several divisions in order that the different lengths may be kept separate.

Use of the spindle (fig. 239). Gold embroidery thread should be wound double upon the spindle. The thread is laid backwards and forwards

Fig. 239. Use of the spindle

above the surface of the fabric, being secured at every turn with two stitches of another, couching, thread. Small holes where the stitches are to come have first to be pierced in the material from the right side. In soft stuffs this is unnecessary but in brocaded materials, and in plush and leather, where every prick shows and would often spoil the whole effect, it is indispensable.

Gold thread which is stiff and difficult to work with can be rendered soft and pliable by putting it into a low oven, or any other warm place, for a short time.

Embroidery with gold purl (fig. 240). Embroidery with gold purl is the easiest kind of gold embroidery. Cut the closely coiled thread into required lengths which you thread like beads on your needle, and

Fig. 240. Embroidery with gold purl

107

fasten them down upon the foundation like the beads in bead-work. Smooth and crimped gold purl, or silver and gold purl used together, look exceedingly well, particularly where the pattern requires effects of light and shade to be reproduced.

Embroidery in diamond stitch (fig. 241). The diamond stitch is a charming novelty in gold embroidery. Short lengths of purl, not more than 1½ mm. long, are threaded on the needle, and the needle is put in and drawn out at the same hole. These stitches form many little glittering knots, turned alternately to the right and left, and look like seed-diamonds in appearance, especially when they are made in silver purl. The shorter the pieces are, and the more closely you set the knots together, the handsomer and richer the effect will be.

Fig. 241. Diamond stitch.

Chinese gold embroidery (figs. 242 and 243). Chinese gold embroidery consists simply in laying down and couching in one or more coloured threads a double gold thread on a delicately outlined pattern, although it can be done on any material, washing or other. This kind of gold embroidery looks especially good on rich fabric such as brocade.

In fig. 242 the trees, foliage and flowers are couched in gold, the grasses in green, the butterflies in red, one of the two birds in dark blue and the other in light blue. Where the design requires it, you may separate the gold threads, and work with one alone.

The second specimen of Chinese embroidery, fig. 243, resembles the first as far as materials and execution are concerned, but the design is different. The grotesque animals, flowers and shells it represents can be worked separately or connected together so as to form a running pattern.

Fig. 242.
Chinese gold
embroidery

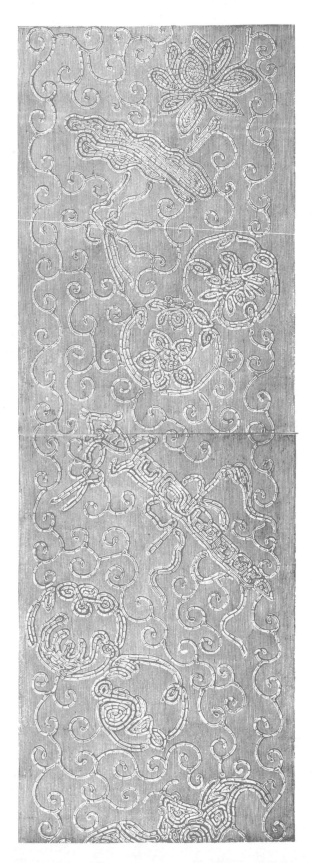

Fig. 243.
Chinese gold
embroidery

Stripe worked in various stitches (fig. 244). All the designs described thus far are worked in the same way but the stripe now presented to our readers introduces them to several kinds of gold thread and a variety of stitches. The small, turned-back petals of the flowers are worked in plain gold thread and outlined with crimped; the rest of the petals are worked in darning stitch, with plain gold thread. The latticed leaves are edged with picots worked with bright purl. The other parts of the design are all worked with a double gold thread, the stalks in dead gold, the leaves in crimped. It looks very well if you use black or red thread for couching the crimped gold and dark or light green for the leaves and tendrils.

Fig. 244. Stripe worked in various stitches

Gold embroidery on a foundation of cords (fig. 245). In the old ecclesiastical embroideries, especially those representing the figures of saints, we often find thick cords used as a foundation, instead of cardboard, for the good reason that the stiff cardboard does not give such soft and rounded contours as a cord foundation which will readily take every bend and turn that you give to it. In the following illustrations we have adhered strictly to the originals as far as the manner of working the surface is concerned, but have substituted for the grey whip cord, which was often used in the past, a white or yellow cord, according to whether it is intended to serve as a foundation to silver or gold work.

Lay and couch as many cords as are necessary to give the design the

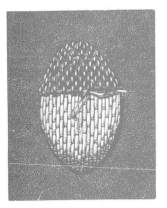 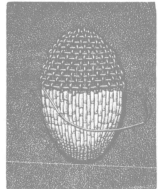 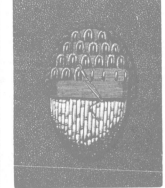

Fig. 245. Embroidery in flattened gold wire and purl

Fig. 246. Plaited stitch in gold purl on a cord foundation

Fig. 247. Scale stitch in gold thread and purl on a cord foundation

requisite thickness, in many cases up to 8 or 10 mm. in height, taking care to lay them closely and solidly in the centre and graduate them down at the sides and ends. When you have finished the foundation, edge it with a thick gold cord, and only then begin the actual embroidery, all the directions just given applying merely to the preparatory work.

Only four of the many stitches that are already in use and might be devised are described here. All are worked on a foundation of vertically laid cords couched with stitches running horizontally. For the pattern represented in fig. 245, flattened gold or silver wire is necessary, cut into pieces long enough to be turned in at the ends so as to form a little loop through which the thread that fastens them down is passed. Over each length of gold or silver wire small lengths of purl are laid at regular intervals, close enough just to leave room for the next stitch, the pieces of one row alternating in position with those of the preceding one.

Plaited stitch in gold purl on a cord foundation (fig. 246). Distribute the stitches as in the previous figure, substituting purl for the flattened gold wire and covering the purl with short lengths of gold thread of the same kind. All these stitches may be worked in gold and silver thread mixed or in the one or the other alone.

Scale stitch worked in gold thread and purl on a cord foundation (fig. 247). Begin by covering much of the padded surface with gold or silver thread laid horizontally, then sew on short lengths of purl, long enough to cover six or eight threads, 2 or 3 mm. apart, as shown in the illustration. These stitches in dead gold purl are then surrounded by shining or crimped purl.

You bring out the working thread to the left of the purl stitch, which you take on your needle, put the needle in on the other side, draw it out above the little stroke and secure the crimped purl with an invisible stitch.

Conventional flower worked on a cord foundation (fig. 248). The half finished flower represented here was copied from a handsome piece of ecclesiastical embroidery enriched with ornament of this kind. The three foregoing stitches and a fourth are employed in its composition. The finished portions on the left hand side are executed in silver and gold purl whilst the egg-shaped heart of the flower is formed of transverse threads carried over the first padding and secured by a stitch between the two cords. In the subsequent row, the catching stitch is set between the cords over which the first gold threads were carried.

The heavier the design is the thicker your padding should be, and cords a good deal thicker than those which are represented in the drawing should be used, as the more light and shade you can introduce into embroidery of this kind the greater will be its beauty and value.

Fig. 248. Conventional flower worked on a cord foundation

Insertion in cross-stitch, alike on both sides, the pattern left blank.

Canvaswork & Linen Embroidery

Canvaswork (also known as Needlepoint or Tapestry) is one of the oldest kinds of needlework and one which has always been popular everywhere.

There are two traditional sorts of canvas in use called, respectively, 'plain (single thread or mono) canvas', and 'Penelope (double thread) canvas'.

Cloth, velvet or plush can also be overlaid with waste canvas, individual threads of which are pulled away after the pattern is finished. For work of this kind we also use a material with less dressing, such as a twisted tammy or Colbert linen, because the pulling out of the harsh rough threads of the canvas is very apt to injure the material beneath.

Stitches worked with waste canvas must be drawn very tight or they will look loose and untidy when the auxiliary fabric is taken away.

Canvaswork should always be done with a square or rectangular frame.

Marking out the embroidery ground (fig. 249). Before beginning a piece of canvaswork and tacking on the auxiliary fabric, count how many stitches it will contain, and mark them out in tens with a coloured thread, as shown in fig. 249, along two sides at least, in the length and breadth. Having ascertained the number of stitches both ways, divide them in two, and starting each time from the middle stitch, trace two lines, one horizontal, the other vertical, right across the canvas. The point of intersection will be the centre. This sort of ground-plan will be found most useful and should not be pulled out until at least half

114

the work be finished. If, moreover, you have corners to work, or a pattern to reverse in the angle of a piece of embroidery, trace a diagonal line besides, from the corner to the centre.

Materials suitable for canvaswork. Hitherto, wool and silk were the materials chiefly used for canvaswork. A very thick wool for carpets was warmer and more durable. Silk is too delicate a fibre to resist much wear and tear and cannot therefore be recommended for articles that are intended for constant use and wool, though stronger, is subject to the destructive agency of moths. Cotton, which is cheaper than both and quite as brilliant, is free from all these disadvantages and is extremely easy to clean.

Cross-stitch (fig. 250). Cross-stitch is the foundation of every other stitch and the one in most common use. It is also called marking-stitch, being used for marking linen. It can be worked in two lines. In the first, the thread is carried diagonally from left to right across a square of threads, and then, downwards, underneath the two horizontal threads; in the second, the stitches are carried from the right-hand lower corner of the square to the upper left-hand corner so that the four points of the two stitches form a perfect square.

Half cross-stitch (fig. 251). If the cotton is too coarse, or the canvas too fine, to make the double stitch, carry the thread back along the whole line and make the half-stitches across it from left to right (this is

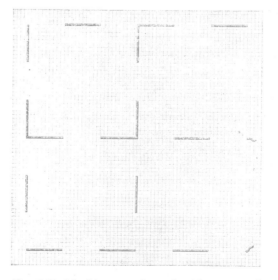

Fig. 249. Marking out the embroidery ground

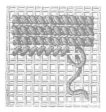  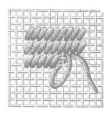

Fig. 250. Cross-stitch   *Fig. 251. Half cross-stitch*   *Fig. 252. Gobelin stitch*

Fig. 253. Gobelin stitch   *Fig. 254. Reps stitch*   *Fig. 255. Tent stitch*
on Penelope canvas

called tramming, and these horizontal lines of thread, horizontal between pairs of double-canvas threads, are already in some pieces bought half-worked, or trammed).

Gobelin stitch on plain canvas (fig. 252). This is worked over two horizontal threads and one vertical. You can work the second row from right to left.

Gobelin stitch on Penelope canvas (fig. 253). For the same stitch on Penelope canvas you need rather a coarse needle which will make its way easily between the threads of the canvas.

Reps stitch (fig. 254). Contrary to Gobelin stitch, this stitch is worked in vertical lines, over two vertical threads and one horizontal one.

Tent or continental stitch (fig. 255). This stitch is simply the first half of a cross or marking-stitch worked over a single thread each way. The illustration shows the working of a row from right to left, the thread being carried forward underneath the vertical threads. Tent stitch, now the most popular canvaswork technique, was in former times used for the most part in conjunction with cross-stitch for the more delicate lines and the shaded parts of flowers and figures.

Wide Gobelin stitch (fig. 256). This stitch covers two vertical and two horizontal threads and advances one thread at a time.

Broad cross-stitch (fig. 257). Worked over two vertical and four horizontal threads (double canvas), and very useful for filling in large

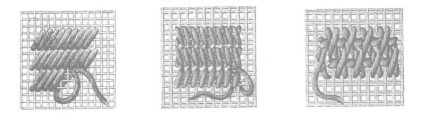

Fig. 256. Wide Gobelin stitch   Fig. 257. Broad cross-stitch   Fig. 258. Double stitch

Fig. 259. Rice stitch   Fig. 260. Plait stitch   Fig. 261. Fern stitch

surfaces as it can be done twice as quickly as the ordinary cross-stitch. It may be varied by turning the crosses first one way and then the other.

Double stitch (fig. 258). Begin with a simple cross-stitch over every alternate intersection of the threads then make a second row of stitches between those of the first, but in this case over two and six threads so that they extend beyond the first each way. In the subsequent rows, a square stitch should be opposed to a long one and a long stitch to a square one.

Rice stitch (crossed-corners cross-stitch) (fig. 259). Fill in the whole ground first with large cross-stitches over four threads each way, then upon these make the so-called rice stitches. These cross the four points of the large cross-stitches and meet in the space between, where they form another cross. The large cross-stitches can be worked in rather coarse cotton, the rice stitches in one of a finer quality.

Plait stitch (fig. 260). This consists of alternate upright and diagonal crosses, worked in rows in two stages.

On double canvas, from the left, go over 4 vertical threads, down vertically under 2 horizontal threads, diagonally up to the right over 4 thread junctions, down under 2 horizontal threads, over 4 vertical threads to the right, and so on, as the bottom line of stitches in the illustration shows. The return journey is worked accordingly.

After you have worked your crosses (thicker thread) you can superimpose more stitches (thin thread).

117

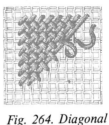

Fig. 262. Stitch for a leaf   *Fig. 263. Fish-bone stitch*   *Fig. 264. Diagonal web stitch*

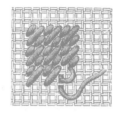

Fig. 265. Cashmere stitch   *Fig. 266. Mosaic stitch*   *Fig. 267. Leviathan stitch*

Fern stitch (fig. 261). Here the stitches are worked in separate rows, over four threads each way. The working thread passes first under the two middle threads, from right to left, and then under the two upper ones, also right to left.

Stitch for a leaf (fig. 262). Carry the thread diagonally over four threads each way, and back under two threads, to the row whence the stitch started. Make rows of back-stitches in a different colour between the rows of diagonals.

Fish-bone stitch (fig. 263). The difference between this and the preceding stitch is that the working thread, after passing diagonally upwards to the right over 6 junctions of threads, is secured by a back-stitch over the last pair of intersections of the canvas threads. These back-stitches lean to the right or left according to the direction of the long stitches.

Diagonal web stitch (fig. 264). Stretch diagonal threads row by row across the whole surface you are going to embroider, and secure each with a row of overcasting stitches. If you are working on Penelope canvas, stitch between the double threads of the canvas. In the next rows the stitches should produce the effect of diagonal or twilled cloth.

Cashmere stitch (fig. 265). To imitate this texture in needlework, first make one stitch over one pair of crossings of the canvas threads, and then two stitches over two pairs of crossings.

Mosaic stitch (fig. 266). Here the thread is carried diagonally first over one and then over two double threads of the canvas.

Leviathan stitch (fig. 267). Also known as double cross-stitch or Smyrna cross-stitch, this consists of an upright on top of a diagonal cross.

Knotted stitch (fig. 268). Carry the working thread over two threads in width and six in height, bring the needle back four threads lower down, in front of the double threads, and insert it behind the preceding stitch, and over the middle threads, and then carry it down to the line of the stitches. In the subsequent rows, the stitches extend over four threads and encroach on two of the previous row so that the stitches of the second row lie between those of the first.

Rococo stitch (figs. 269, 270, 271). After fastening in your thread, lay it vertically over four single or two double threads, as the case may be, and carry the needle through to the left, under one double thread; then, as fig. 269 shows, bring it back over the first stitch, put it in by the side of it, and bring it out below, under half the horizontal threads covered by the first stitch. Then make a stitch to the right, similar to the one just made to the left.

When you have finished one stitch, carry the needle under one thread, in an oblique line, to the next stitch, see fig. 270. The whole pattern is here worked in diagonal lines.

Parisian stitch (fig. 272). This stitch makes a very good grounding in cases where the material is not intended to be completely hidden. It

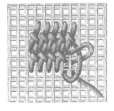

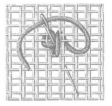

Fig. 268. Knotted stitch

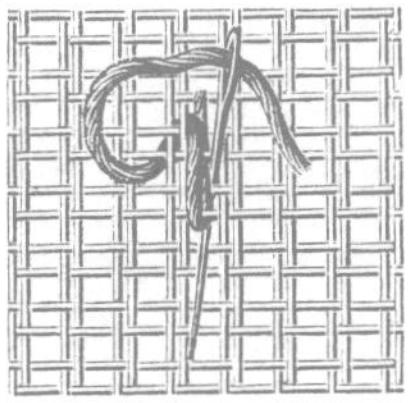

Fig. 269. Rococo stitch. First stitches on the wrong side.

Fig. 270. Rococo stitch. Stitches on the right side.

Fig. 271. Rococo stitch. Completed.

119

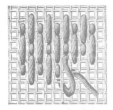

Fig. 272. Parisian stitch

Fig. 273. Greek stitch

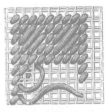

Fig. 274. Scotch stitch

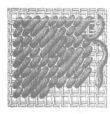

Fig. 275. Moorish stitch

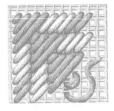

Fig. 276. Oriental stitch

Fig. 277. Shell stitch

consists of a long vertical stitch over three pairs of threads, and a short stitch over one pair, alternately.

Greek stitch (fig. 273). This differs from the ordinary cross-stitch in the oblique inclination given to the threads, and the manner in which it is begun. After the first stitch you bring your needle back from right to left, under the vertical threads of the first stitch, carry it diagonally downwards to a distance of four threads beyond the first stitch then right to left under the vertical threads of this stitch. The next stitch is made like the first. The rows may be joined together either by the short or the long stitches but you must follow one rule throughout. This stitch is much used in Slavonic countries for the adornment of linen garments, and there we have observed that the short stitches are generally made to encounter the long ones.

Scotch stitch (fig. 274). Squares, composed of slanting stitches made over one, three, five, three threads or pairs of threads, and separated from each other by vertical and horizontal rows of tent stitches, constitute what is ordinarily known by the name of Scotch stitch.

Moorish stitch (fig. 275). For this stitch, instead of surrounding squares of stitches, as in Scotch stitch, the squares are made to touch, rising like steps one above the other, separated by steps of tent stitch.

Oriental stitch (fig. 276). Here you make four diagonal stitches over one, two, three and four double threads respectively which form triangles one above the other. The empty spaces between are filled up with tent stitches covering two threads.

Shell stitch (fig. 277). Carry your thread upwards over six horizontal threads, then from right to left under one vertical thread and downwards over six horizontal ones. When you have made four vertical stitches in this way, bring the needle out between the third and fourth stitches, and fasten the four long stitches together with a back-stitch to the middle thread of the canvas. Draw a thread of a different colour twice through these back-stitches so as to form small coils, like shells, and then fill in the ground between the rows of long stitches with back-stitches.

Jacquard stitch (fig. 278). If you have a large plain surface to cover you can choose a stitch that forms a pattern in itself. Jacquard stitch is one of many such stitches illustrated here. To work Jacquard stitch, make six stitches underneath one another over two double threads, and six by the side of one another, from left to right, over two double threads. The second row consists of the same number of tent stitches, similarly worked downwards and to the side.

Byzantine stitch (fig. 279). Here you make the same number of stitches as in the preceding figure but each row of stitches is made either over four threads or two pairs of threads.

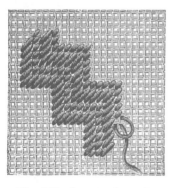

Fig. 278. Jacquard stitch

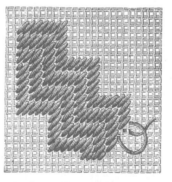

Fig. 279. Byzantine stitch

Milanese stitch (fig. 280). Alternating triangles are here formed by diagonal rows of back-stitches, firstly over one and four, then (twice) over two and three, and lastly over four and one, junction of threads or pair of threads, as illustrated. The last long stitches of each triangle should come under the last short ones and the short ones in the middle of the last long ones.

Plush stitch (fig. 281). This stitch, also called Astrachan or velvet stitch, by means of which a very good imitation of an Oriental rug can be produced, consists of loops, each secured by a cross-stitch. The

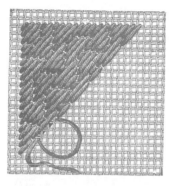

Fig. 280. Milanese stitch

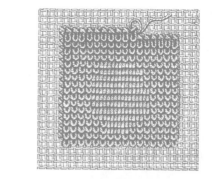

Fig. 281. Plush stitch

best way to ensure these loops being even and regular is to make them over a pencil.

The effect can be varied by cutting the loops, which gives the surface the appearance of velvet.

The illustration represents only the middle loops cut, for the cut and the uncut stitch can both be introduced into the same piece of embroidery. For example, the borders in figs. 285 and 286 are worked in open or cut plush stitch whilst in the centres the stitch is left uncut.

To make a row of stitches, take the thread over your pencil (not shown in illustration) and work a binding cross-stitch over the loop's exit from and entry to the canvas. Make a similar stitch immediately adjacent, and so on. Remove the pencil when you have completed a row and work another row above.

Knitting stitch (fig. 282). In old collections we often meet with very interesting pieces of needlework used for hangings or screens,

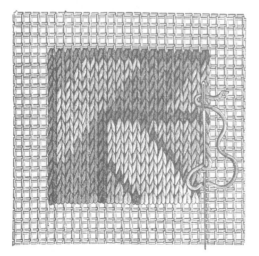

Fig. 282. Knitting stitch

executed in vertical rows of chain stitch on canvas. Patterns in many colours gain immensely by being worked in this stitch as the colours blend together better than in any other, and even the shape of the stitch contributes to soften the contrasts of colour.

The stitch is worked as follows; after fastening in your thread, insert the needle at the same hole it came out of, and bring it out two threads, or pairs of threads, above. Keep the loop formed by the working thread under the point of the needle. The thread should not be drawn up tightly but left to form a rather loose, round loop. For the next stitches, insert the needle close to the thread that issues from the last loop.

Pattern for borders or grounding (fig. 283). This simple but most effective design copied from one of the most beautiful of Oriental carpets, can be executed in either cross-stitch, plush stitch or knitting stitch. To make a wider border still, the diagonal lines that divide the figures shaped like an S have only to be prolonged, and the figures repeated.

The colours have been chosen with the view of reproducing as nearly as possible the subdued and faded tones, which time has imparted to the original.

Pattern for grounding (fig. 284). Diagonal lines, intersected by bosses, serve here as a setting for quaintly shaped flowers and leaves. The outlines are all worked in cross-stitch, and the solid parts in either tent stitch or Gobelin stitch.

Fig. 283. Pattern for borders or grounding. Colour chart: ◨ *bright red 349,* ⊠ *deep red 902,* ▣ *indigo blue 311,* □ *indigo blue 939,* ⊡ *ash grey 414,* ▨ *old gold 725,* ◪ *moss green 470.*

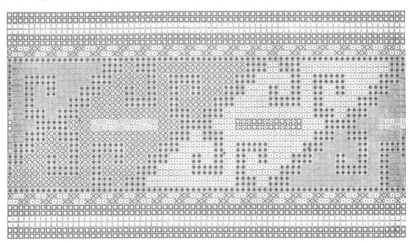

Fig. 284. Pattern for grounding. Colour chart: ■ *black 310,* ▧ *ochre 676,* ▦ *dull cinnamon 315,* ▨ *scarlet 349,* ▥ *sunrise 352,* ⊠ *indigo 311,* ⊡ *pale blue 775,* ✶ *deep red 902,* ▧ *grey-green 501,* ◧ *grey-green 500.*

Part of a design suitable for carpets (figs. 285 and 286). Our space will not admit of our reproducing more than a quarter of this design. Colours of the softest shades should be selected for it. A black line divides the pattern into four quarters. The upper quarter on the right and the lower one on the left should be worked in blue, and the upper one on the left copied from fig. 286.

The narrow border, in red, blue and green, is to be repeated after the broad band, which is represented in fig. 285, has been added to the grounding. A very good effect is obtained if in the broad border, fig. 285, you vary the background of the different subjects.

Linen embroidery. Some stitches used in linen embroidery are very similar to those used in canvas work. The ordinary cross-stitch, as represented in fig. 250, is the one most commonly used, but it is not so effective from the wrong side as the two-sided stitches, which in the beautiful old needlework of the fifteenth, sixteenth and seventeenth centuries have always excited our wonder and admiration.

Stuffs suitable for linen embroidery. Most embroidery of this kind, and more especially the Italian, is done on very evenweave linen with clearly definable warp and weft threads, in the holes between which

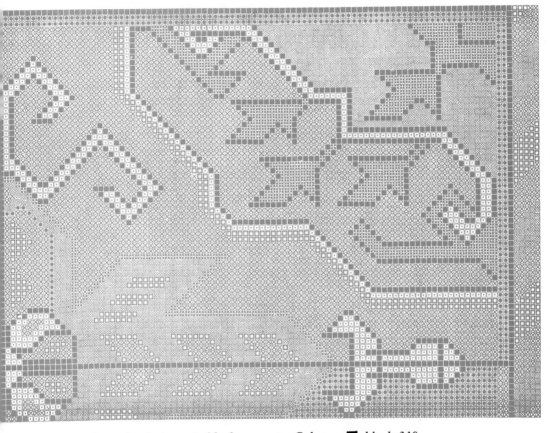

Fig. 285. Part of a design suitable for carpets. Colours: ■ black 310, ⊠ pomegranate 900, ✚ deep red 902, ▦ indigo 311, ▧ blue 322, ✪ soft green 470, ⊡ taupe 451.

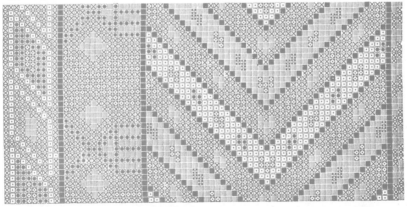

Fig. 286. Outer border of the design for carpets fig. 285. Colours: ■ black 310, ⊠ pomegranate 900, ◈ deep red 902, ◆ indigo 311, ▥ old gold 3045, ◨ soft green 470, ✚ taupe 451.

the needle is passed. In addition to the finer kinds of linen, a great variety of textures are now manufactured that can be easily counted. Many people today work on Glenshee linen; others prefer to work on Aida and Hardanger cloths, forming stitches over blocks of threads.

Linen fabrics are generally white, unbleached or cream-coloured. All three are used for embroidery but the coloured cottons show up best on the cream ground; on the white, they look hard and crude, and on the unbleached, dull and faded.

Threads suitable for linen embroidery. As some linen embroidery is executed on articles that are subjected to frequent washing, the DMC stranded cottons (*Mouliné spécial*, often called floss), which are to be had in every shade and colour, are the best for the purpose. For coarse stuffs, coarse cotton such as Coton à broder should be used. Finer threads such as one strand of six-stranded cotton or a complete thickness of DMC Machine Embroidery Twist, should be used for the finer stuffs.

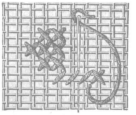

Fig. 287. Plain cross-stitch on auxiliary canvas

Plain cross-stitch on auxiliary canvas (fig. 287). Plain cross-stitch, commonly called marking-stitch, has already been described in fig. 250. But it may be well to observe that when an auxiliary material such as waste canvas is used it should be most carefully tacked upon the stuff following the thread of the same, and a sufficient margin left to allow of the drawing out of the canvas threads when the work is finished.

Two-sided cross-stitch (also sometimes called marking stitch), worked in four rows of stitches (figs. 288, 289, 290). Straight lines of cross-stitch alike on both sides, can be worked in two journeys to and fro. Working from left to right, begin by fastening in your thread, never with a knot, but by two or three little running stitches which are hidden afterwards by your first cross-stitch. Directing your needle to the right, pass it diagonally over a double cross of the warp and woof of the canvas and so on to the end of the line.

Having reached the last stitch, draw out your thread in the middle

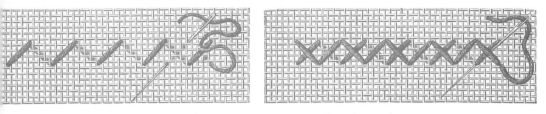

*Fig. 288. First half of the first journey
and auxiliary stitch for returning*

*Fig. 289. One journey and first half of the second
finished, and auxiliary stitch leading
to the second return.*

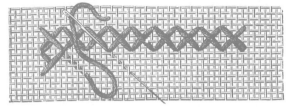

*Fig. 290. The two journeys to and fro, completing
one row of cross-stitch, both sides alike.*

of it, make an auxiliary diagonal stitch downwards to the right, bring
the needle up in the middle of the last stitch, take it thence upwards to
the left, across two threads, and begin the return journey, from right
to left, crossing and thus completing the first row of stitches. In the
auxiliary stitch with which you begin the backward journey the thread
lies double on both sides.

Two-sided cross-stitch (figs. 291 and 292). The above mode of working

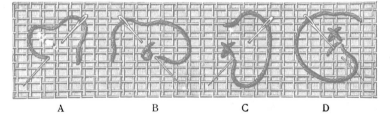

A   B   C   D

Fig. 291. Two-sided cross-stitch. Different positions of the needle.

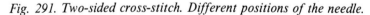

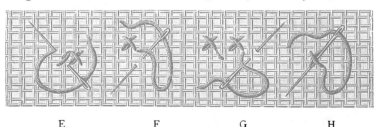

E   F   G   H

Fig. 292. Two-sided cross-stitch. Different positions of the needle.

two-sided cross-stitch cannot be applied to letters, or patterns in broken lines, which both consist chiefly of isolated stitches. Figs. 291 and 292 explain the course of the stitches in embroidery of this kind.

The working detail A, fig. 291, indicates the spot for the thread to enter the stuff and the position of the needle for the first and second stitches; B illustrates the first two stitches completed, with an auxiliary stitch to the right, the thread drawn out on the right, and the position of the needle for the stitch that completes the cross; C shows the completion of the stitch begun at B and the position of the needle for a second stitch to the right.

D (fig. 291) shows one cross-stitch completed and another begun, in this instance, immediately beneath A. In fig. 292, E shows how to work stitches to the left; F illustrates an auxiliary stitch to reach an isolated cross-stitch on the right, G, auxiliary stitches between two isolated cross-stitches, and H, a second and last auxiliary stitch to complete the cross.

It requires both practice and care to do this two-sided cross-stitch so as not to disfigure the stuff by superfluous stitches.

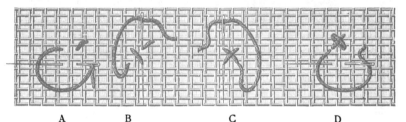

A   B   C   D

Fig. 293. Right side of the cross-stitch, forming a square at the back.

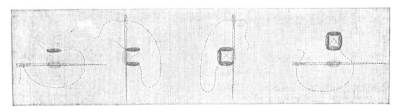

Fig. 294. Square stitch forming the back of the cross-stitch.

Cross-stitch forming a square at the back (figs. 293 and 294). Many of the alphabets we so admire in old samplers are worked in cross-stitch that forms a square at the back. Each stitch has to be finished off before another is begun; if you carefully examine figs. 293 and 294, which show the right and the wrong sides of the stitch, you will find no difficulty in mastering it. Letter A, fig. 293, shows the entrance of the thread, the position of the needle for half the cross-stitch on the right

Fig. 295. Two-sided Italian stitch.
*Introduction of the thread and position
of the needle for the first stitch.*

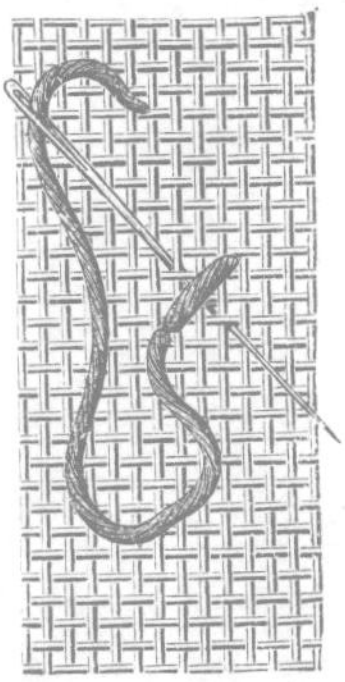

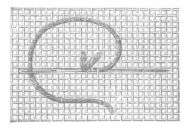

Fig. 296. Two-sided Italian stitch.
*Position of the needle for
the 2nd and 3rd stitches.*

Fig. 297. Two-sided Italian stitch.
*Position of the needle for the
4th and 5th stitches.*

Fig. 298. Two-sided
*Italian stitch. Return
journey, which completes
the cross-stitch.*

side, and the second side of the square at the back, as shown in fig. 294, A. Letter B, fig. 293, shows the cross-stitch finished and the position of the needle for the third side of the square on the wrong side, indicated by the same letter in fig. 294. C, in both figures, indicates a stitch which is double on the right side and on the wrong side forms the fourth side of the square, whilst letter D explains how to continue with another stitch beneath this stitch.

Two-sided Italian stitch (figs. 295, 296, 297, 298). Two-sided Italian stitch consists of cross-stitches, alike on both sides, divided from each other by horizontal and vertical stitches. The upper diagonal of each stitch should all slope one way, as in plain cross-stitch.

Italian stitch is worked in one journey. Fig. 295 shows how to fasten in the thread and place the needle for the first stitch, from right to left; fig. 296 the position of the needle from left to right to form the cross at the back and the vertical stitch on the right side; fig. 297 shows the position of the needle for a two-sided horizontal stitch at the bottom of the cross, after which you proceed as in fig. 295. Fig. 298 explains the return journey, which completes each cross.

On a thin stuff this stitch produces an extremely pretty effect,

129

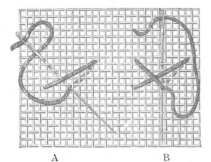

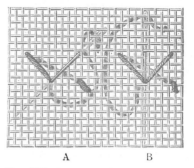

Fig. 299. Montenegrin cross-stitch.
1st, 2nd, 3rd, 4th and 5th stitch
and transversal stitch.

Fig. 300. Montenegrin cross-stitch.
Position of the stitches on the wrong side.

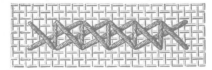

Fig. 301. Montenegrin cross-stitch. A row of stitches finished.

resembling lattice-work, provided the thread be tightly drawn in the working.

Montenegrin cross-stitch (figs. 299, 300, 301). The Slavonic tribes of the southern districts of E. Europe, especially the Montenegrins, have a great partiality for this stitch, which has been rarely noticed hitherto in books on needlework. The right side shows cross-stitches with a double thread underneath and divided by vertical stitches, the wrong side, regular cross-stitches also divided by vertical stitches. Coarse thread, or several strands of stripped, stranded cotton, should be used for this stitch; it produces a richer effect and not only covers the stuff better, but also hides the underneath stitch, which in the Slavonic work is entirely hidden by the cross-stitches.

Begin, as letter A indicates, with a long, slanting stitch, across over twice as many vertical as horizontal threads then, bringing your needle back from right to left, back diagonally downwards, draw it out, carry it over diagonally the first long stitch, and insert it again diagonally from left to right (A, fig. 299). These four stages finished, proceed to the fifth and sixth, which as B shows cross the first four then repeat the first stitch.

The threads that form the stitches on the wrong side should always be opposed to each other, that is, one cross should lean to the right and the next to the left, as shown in fig. 300. This variation in the inclination of the stitches, which is regarded as a fault in plain cross-stitch, is indispensable here and produces a charming effect on the wrong side.

Plaited Algerian stitch (fig. 302). This is really a close herring-bone stitch. Horizontal stitches, always from right to left, are formed alternately at the top and bottom of a row.

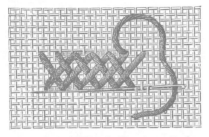

Fig. 302. Plaited Algerian stitch

Two-sided Spanish plaited stitch (figs. 303 and 304). This stitch has the advantage of being not only very effective but also very quickly executed. It is worked in two rows, forwards and backwards, as shown in figs. 303 and 304.

Diagonal line stitch (figs. 305 and 306). Diagonal line, square stitch or faggot as it is sometimes called, requires practice to make the

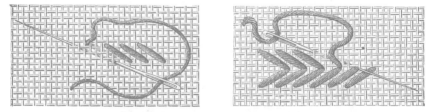

Fig. 303. Two-sided plaited Spanish stitch Fig. 304.

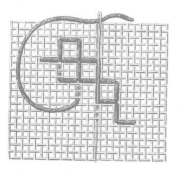
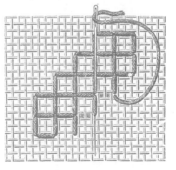

Fig. 305. Diagonal line stitch. Forward row.   *Fig. 306. Backward row.*

131

stitches follow in their proper order. Fig. 305 explains how the needle has to pass, alternately, step by step, over and under the threads of the stuff, and fig. 306 shows how the threads left blank the first time are covered on the way back. The great difficulty is how to place your first row of stitches so as to ensure an unbroken course back. It is as well before setting out to ascertain clearly the most direct course back so that you may not come to a stand-still, or be obliged to make unnecessary stitches on the wrong side. If you have to pass obliquely across the stuff, as in patterns figs. 321, 322, 323, 324, proceed in the same way as though you were covering the straight threads of a fabric.

Two-sided insertion (figs. 307, 308, 309, 310, 311, 312, 313). We conclude this series of stitches with a description of a pretty, two-sided insertion suitable for joining stripes of work of different widths together. In pieces of old needlework, we often find handsome coloured patterns joined together by a piece of lace or some quite different kind of work. The insertion shown in fig. 312 is a very good substitute for either. Figs. 307, 308, 309, 310 and 311 show stages of this stitch. Fig. 313 shows the back of the work, which though quite a different pattern will combine very well with any two-sided embroidery.

These insertions can be worked on any stuff but the stitches must be done, both ways, on a number of threads divisible by 3. Thus, the first stitch may cover 6, 9 or 12 threads but never 8, 10 or 14.

Two-sided insertion   Fig. 307. First detail   *Fig. 308. Second detail*

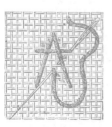
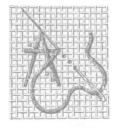
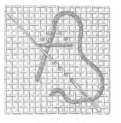

Fig. 309. Third detail   *Fig. 310. Fourth detail*   *Fig. 311. Fifth detail*

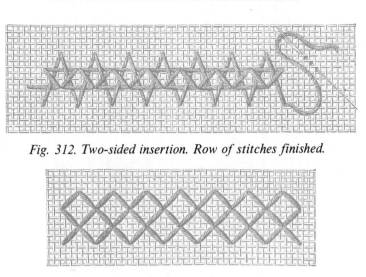

Fig. 312. Two-sided insertion. Row of stitches finished.

Fig. 313. Two-sided insertion, showing the back of fig. 312.

Gothic borders in tent or cross-stitch (figs. 314 and 315). We are indebted for both these pretty patterns, which are quite Gothic in their character, to a visit we paid to the national museum at Munich

Fig. 314. Gothic border in cross-stitch. Colours: Turkish red 321 or two values of indigo blue, 311 and 334, or two values of pomegranate, 900 and 947, or two values of mahogany, 300 and 402.

where we discovered them amongst a heap of other old valuables lying un-heeded in a remote corner. Their simple graceful outlines render them peculiarly suitable for the decoration of table-cloths, counter-panes, curtains, etc. All embroideries of this kind should be finished off with a deep fringe made in the stuff itself or knotted on to it, or may be trimmed with a heavy thread lace, of a wide width, corresponding with the work in character.

The design may be worked either in one shade, as in fig. 314, or in two, as in fig. 315, where all the outside stitches are worked in the darker shade of the given colours.

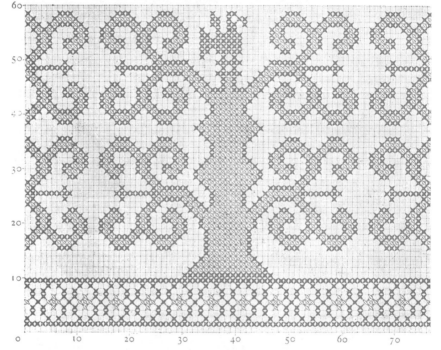

Fig. 315. Gothic border in cross-stitch. Colours: Indigo blue 311 and 334, or Cardinal red 606 and geranium 353, or lime green 699 and 704

Powdering and border. Albanian subjects (figs. 316 and 317). The arrangement of colours for these charming patterns, of Albanian origin, should be as follows; the dark-coloured crosses, red, the lighter ones alternately blue and green, the lightest, yellow.

In fig. 316, most of the stitches in every other diagonal row are worked in red, the others in green or blue; in the intermediate rows the flowers are worked alternately in green and red or blue and red, and, throughout, the centre of each figure should consist of 4 stitches in yellow.

134

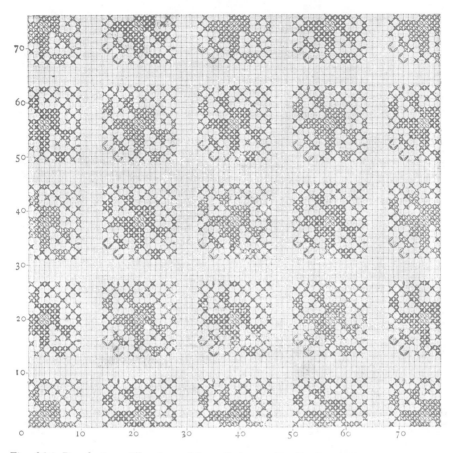

Fig. 316. Powdering. Albanian subject. Colours: Cardinal red 606, indigo blue 322, green 470, sunflower yellow 444, taupe 451.

In fig. 317, which serves as a border to the above, only the stalks of the four stylized florets, radiating from the central cross, are in brown.

These squares are separated from the bottom border by an insertion, in tent stitch, worked over 6 threads, in red, blue, green and yellow, from 20 to 25 stitches of each. This band is edged on both sides with a row of stem stitches worked in yellow over 4 threads. The Holbein stitches that border the band can be made in whichever colour the worker prefers, or else in red and gold thread.

Borders in back- or double-running stitch (figs. 318, 319, 320). These three patterns will give our readers an opportunity of perfecting themselves in back- or double-running stitch (see figs. 305 and 306), also called Holbein, stroke or line stitch.

135

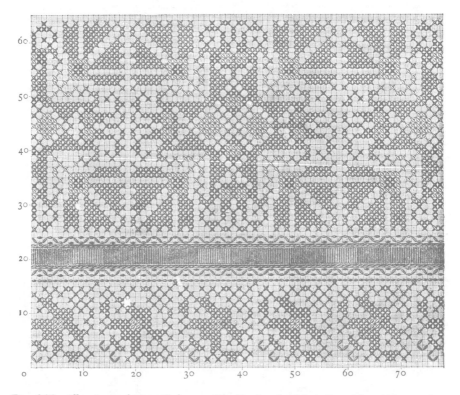

Fig. 317. Albanian subject. Colours: Cardinal red 606, indigo blue 311, sunflower yellow 444, green 470, taupe 451.

We again recommend our readers to begin by ascertaining the course the stitches should take, in order to avoid all unnecessary stitches and be sure of finding their way back according to the prescribed rule.

Corners in back-stitch (figs. 321 and 322). These pretty little patterns are suitable for the decoration of ladies' and children's collars, fine pocket-handkerchiefs and finger napkins, and can be worked in one or two colours as preferred. If two colours be used, the darker should be taken for the interior, the lighter for the narrow outside edge.

Stripe in back-stitch (fig. 323). This is copied from a piece of Italian work, though from a resemblance in the different subjects to the rose, thistle and shamrock it might have been supposed to be of English origin. The original work was executed in a most brilliant purple red which time has toned down to the colour of soft red 309 or leather brown 433, one or other of which we recommend.

Fig. 318. Border in back- or double-running stitch. Colours: Turkish red 321 or indigo blue 311.

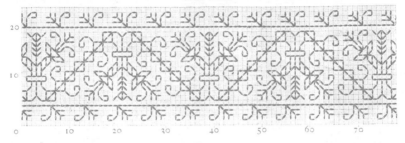

Fig. 319. Border in back- or double-running stitch. Colours: dark green 319 or moss green 470.

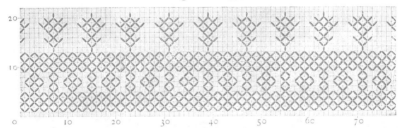

Fig. 320. Insertion in back- or double-running stitch. Colours: Turkish red 321 or soft red 309 or indigo blue 311.

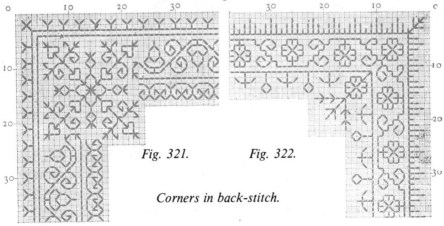

Fig. 321.   *Fig. 322.*

Corners in back-stitch.

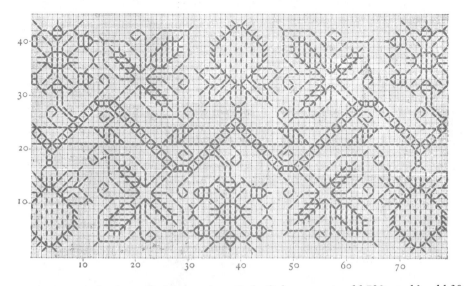

Fig. 323. Stripe in back- or double-running stitch. Colours: rust gold 729 or old gold 3045.

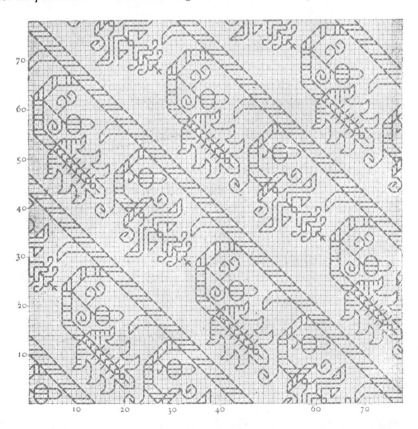

Fig. 324. Grounding in diagonal lines. Colours: indigo blue 322 or Cardinal red 606.

138

Grounding in diagonal lines (fig. 324). This pattern can be worked in back-stitch or double-running stitch. It is only suitable for large surfaces on account of the diagonal lines and should be worked all in one colour. It can be varied by adding sprays to the upper sides of the slanting stalks, like those on the lower sides, turned either the same way or upwards. Skilled workers will readily contrive the middles for themselves, by combining the different subjects and putting them together in various positions, either diagonally or at right angles to each other.

Powdering in cross-, back- and double-running stitch (fig. 325). This charming combination of stitches can be made use of wherever embroidery is available as a means of decoration.

Fig. 325. Powdering in cross-, back- or double-running stitch. Colours: for the cross-stitches, pomegranate 900, for the back- or double-running stitches indigo blue 311 and golden 783.

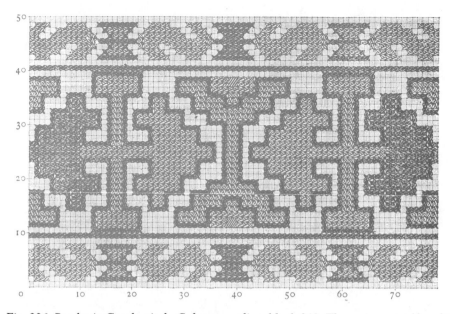

Fig. 326. Border in Greek stitch. Colours: outline, black 310. The main central band is worked in two greens (say, 3348 and 3345), the 'S's are worked in French blue 342 and the motifs between in two reds (say, 321 and 902) and yellow, 307.

Border in Greek stitch (fig. 326). This attractive design is outlined in black. The vertical 'poles' of the central band are worked with the fabric turned through 90°.

Grounding (fig. 327). This grounding was copied from a beautiful old cushion-cover and will be found particularly useful in the confection of small embroidered articles because the pattern will always form a centre point in itself. A red, such as either of the two colours indicated beneath the figure, will best reproduce the tone of the original.

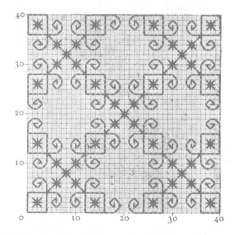

Fig. 327. Grounding. Colours: red 606 or deep peony 3687.

140

In making the little stars that connect the different squares, the mode we recommend is coming up on the *outside* of each star and taking your needle back in through the shared central hole. This will produce a much crisper star.

Wallachian border (fig. 328). A piece of Wallachian needlework executed on rough linen and uncommon both in colour and design

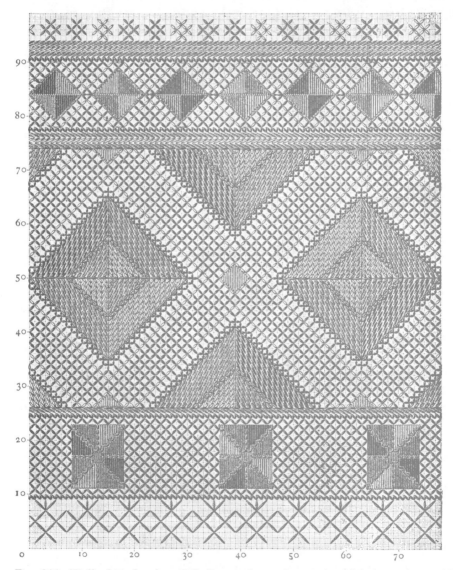

Fig. 328. Wallachian border. Gobelin stitch, stroke stitch and halves of two-sided Spanish plaited stitch. Colours: Cardinal red 606, geranium 352, pistachio 966 and old gold 3046.

141

suggested the charming embroidery here. In place of the somewhat violent colours, which indicate an undeveloped taste, we have substituted softer and more refined ones. All the back-stitches of the middle stripe and of the two border stripes, top and bottom, as well as the darker portions of the small dice, subdivided into eight, in the bottom border, and of the small diagonal squares in the top border, worked in Gobelin stitch, are in red, colour 344. The setting of upright back-stitches round the large centre figures, as well as the straight lines that divide these same figures into four, are worked in yellow.

The squares and the half-squares are worked in geranium, pistachio and old gold thread: geranium is indicated in the illustration by the darkest shade, pistachio by the medium shade, and the old gold thread by the lightest shade.

The stitches in the right bottom quarter and top left one incline upwards from left to right, in the two other quarters they incline the contrary way. The single rows of two-sided Spanish plaited stitch as shown in fig. 304 can only be done over 4 and 2 threads and worked one way, not to and fro.

The general effect is very much heightened by the introduction of one or two rows of stitches, worked in old gold thread, into the straight lines on either side of the stripes; all the light parts of the design, moreover, should be worked in old gold thread.

Borders in several shades of one colour (figs. 329 and 330). In some beautifully embroidered Chinese hangings that latterly came under our notice, the principal subject was the figure of a mandarin in a very richly decorated dress. The pretty pattern given in fig. 329, was copied from the collar and cuffs of this dress.

The border of these hangings furnished us with pattern 330, which will be found to look best worked in three very distinct shades of blue.

The grotesque heads of animals, and the flowers and branches which break the running pattern and are a Chinese speciality, distinguish this design from the more conventional patterns of the present day.

We recommend these two pretty patterns as likewise adaptable by transposition to centres, or by repetition to broad stripes. With very little trouble they can be converted into a variety of subjects such as it is often difficult to find ready made and exactly suited to the purpose in hand.

Border in Greek stitch (fig. 331). This design can be worked in Greek, Montenegrin or plaited Algerian stitch. Our illustration, worked in

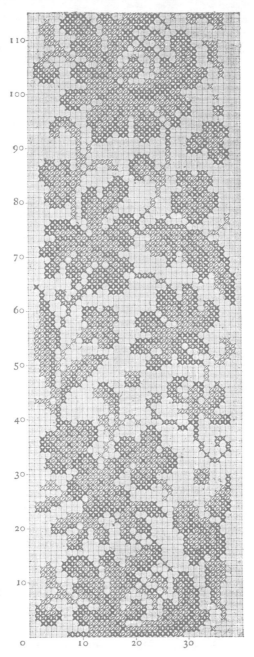

Fig. 329. Border in several shades of one colour. Colours: three shades of either indigo blue, geranium or purple.

Greek stitch, shows how one stitch encroaches upon another and how the thread is carried from one isolated stitch to another.

143

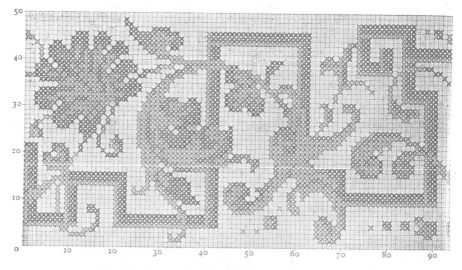

Fig. 330. Border in several shades of one colour

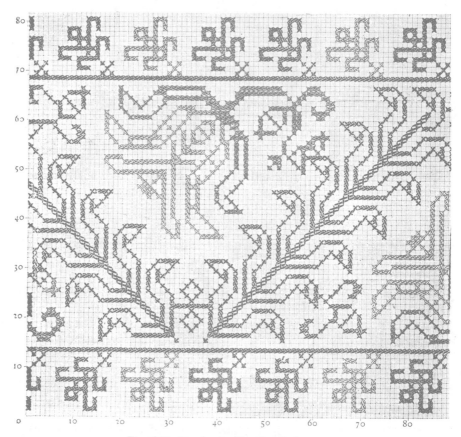

Fig. 331. Border in Greek stitch

It will be found to be an improvement if the stitches are so made as to follow the direction of the lines. The central subject may be repeated two or three times according to the width of border required. The edging is the same throughout.

Table-cover in satin and back- or double-running stitch (figs. 332, 333, 334, 335). This tasteful little table-cover provides excellent practice in working satin stitches which, set very closely, unite and form a star in the centre of the principal subject. Other blocks of satin stitch form leaves, set in diagonal rows radiating to the centre of the design. Each row of leaves has similar colouring. The outermost leaf is deep red; thereafter leaves are, in repeating order, in green, violet and blue; the little branches in back-stitch, on each side of the satin stitches, correspond with them in colour, and the small figures that form the border of the square may be worked indiscriminately in any of the colours used for the satin stitches of the centre. Fig. 335 shows the whole design, and fig. 332 can be seen appearing twice in the central area. The satin stitches of fig. 332 should be pistachio, the surrounding stitches lees red. All other motifs in this main central area can be rust yellow.

The wide border consists of stars, alternately deep red and indigo blue, pistachio or rust yellow. Dividing lines between and around stars, and the hooked patterns on the inside and outside of this whole border, can be deep red or indigo. If you wish strictly to adhere to the pattern, a fine linen will be the best material to select, with one strand of DMC stranded cotton for the back- or double-running stitches and two strands of stripped DMC stranded cotton for the satin.

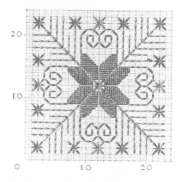

Fig. 332. Small detached subject of fig. 335

Fig. 333. Outer border of fig. 335

Fig. 334. Middle of fig. 335

147

Fig. 335. Table-cover in satin and back- or double-running stitch. Colours: deep red 902, pistachio 966, lees red 315, rust yellow 729 and indigo blue 322.

Appliqué work on satin set with fine cord

Miscellaneous Fancy Work

Knotted cord (figs. 336, 337, 338, 339, 340). In making knotted cord the fingers take the place of a crochet needle.

You tie two ends of thread or braid together, take one thread in the left hand, fig. 336, and with the forefinger of the right pull out a loop long enough for the left forefinger to pass through and hold the end of the thread tight with the little finger of the right hand.

Then draw the left forefinger backwards through the loop and behind the thread that is round the loop and lies in the left hand, fig. 337. As you lay the thread round the left forefinger, you must pass the knot and the ends of thread as well over into the left hand, and with the right hand pull the thread that lies on the right and draw up the loop, fig. 338.

In fig. 339, representing the fourth position of the hands, you are shown how the forefinger of the right hand lifts up the thread and passes through the loop on the left hand; the end will consequently also pass immediately into the right hand and the left hand will tighten the knot.

It is by thus drawing up first a loop on the right and then one on the left that this pretty cord is produced.

Skilful hands will soon learn to make a cord of the same kind with four threads, as follows: knot the four ends of thread together, make a few knots, using two threads as one, then dropping the loop on your forefinger, put the next one upon it and draw up the knot, passing, however, the threads over those that you dropped. Then drop the loop you have on your finger again and take up the first loops.

Fig. 340. Knotted cord

Fig. 336. Knotted cord.
First position of the hands.

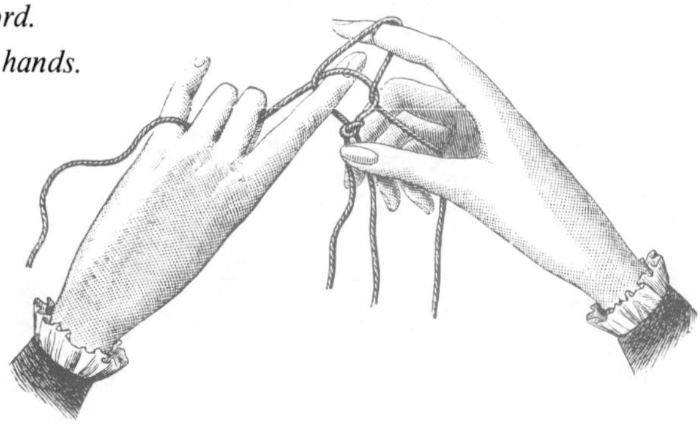

Fig. 337.
Second position of the hands.

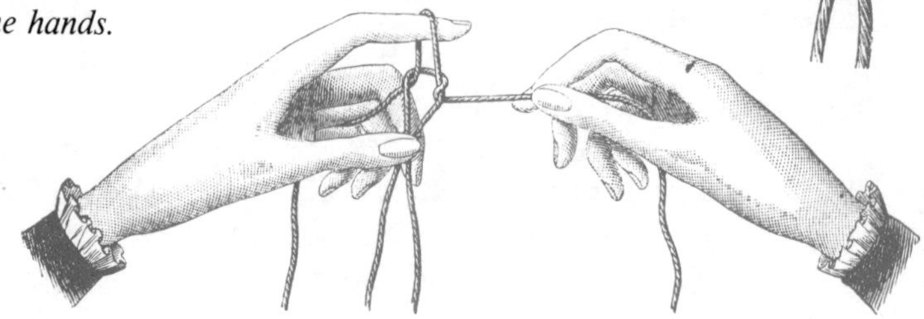

Fig. 338.
Third position of the hands.

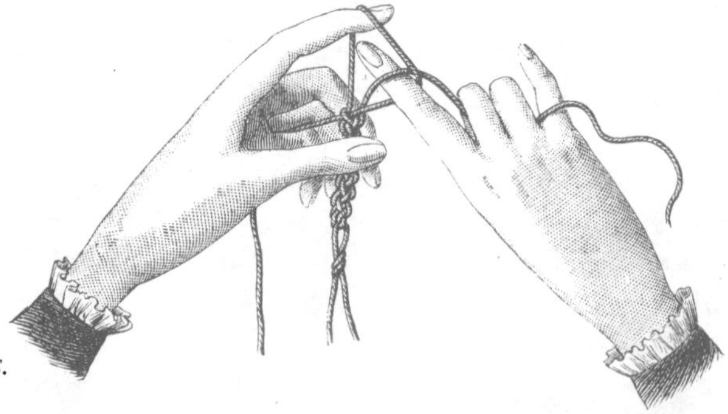

Fig. 339.
Fourth position of the hands.

Balls for trimmings (figs. 341, 342, 343, 344, 345, 346). To make these, begin by cutting a number of rounds of cardboard, two for every ball, with holes in the middle, fig. 341.

If you have a great many balls to make it is well worth your while providing yourself with a metal die of the proper size, to cut the rounds with.

150

Lay two of these rounds together and cover them closely with stitches, fig. 342.

When the round is entirely covered, put the scissors in between the two circles of cardboard and cut open the stitches all round the outer edge, fig. 343; then draw a piece of thread between the two circles and knot it firmly round the stitches that meet in the centre hole, fig. 344; leave sufficiently long ends of thread hanging to form a loop by which the ball can afterwards be fastened to the heading of the fringe; when the stitches are knotted together you cut and pull out the cardboard, fig. 345, and snip the thread with your scissors until it becomes quite fluffy and the ball is perfectly round, as shown in fig. 346.

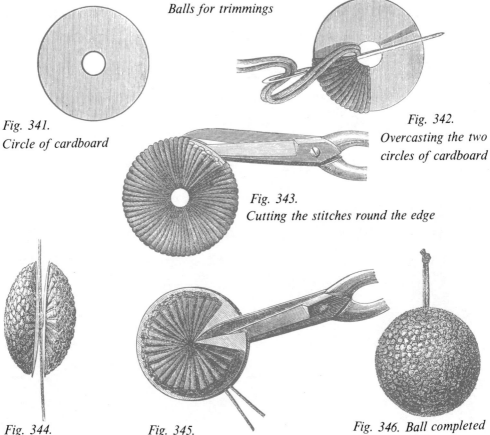

Balls for trimmings

Fig. 341.
Circle of cardboard

Fig. 342.
Overcasting the two circles of cardboard

Fig. 343.
Cutting the stitches round the edge

Fig. 344.
Putting in the loop

Fig. 345.
Cutting out the cardboard

Fig. 346. Ball completed
with loop attached

Tambour work (figs. 347, 348, 349, 350). Since the introduction of the sewing machine, by means of which this charming kind of embroidery can be so quickly and easily executed, it has somewhat gone out of

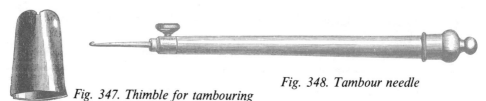

Fig. 347. Thimble for tambouring

Fig. 348. Tambour needle

favour. As, however, the fine patterns with a good deal of shading in them can be far more accurately worked by hand than by machine, tambouring, which is in point of fact merely a form of crochet on cloth, producing a continuous line of chain stitch on the front of the work, has lately been revived. The piece of stuff on which the tambour work is to be done must be mounted on a frame.

The loops are made with a small hook called a tambour needle, and they must be regular and even; to facilitate this a sort of thimble, fig.

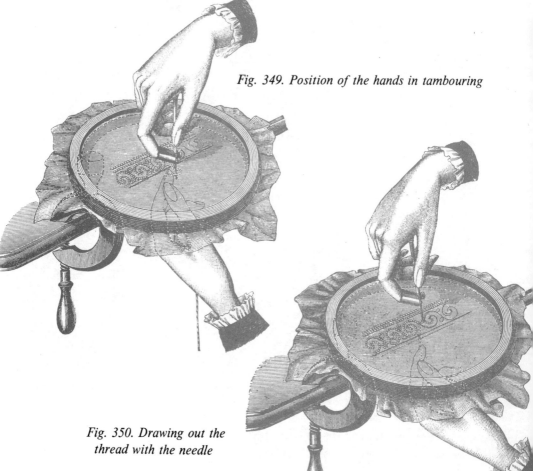

Fig. 349. Position of the hands in tambouring

Fig. 350. Drawing out the thread with the needle

347, is worn on the forefinger of the right hand, formed of a small plate of sheet brass, rolled up but not joined so as to fit any finger; it is open at the top like a tailor's thimble and has a little notch on the side which is placed above the nail, and in which you lay the tambour needle whilst you work. From the thimble being cut slightly slanting at the top, it follows that the inside where the two ends meet is a little shorter than the outside.

The thread, held underneath the fabric, is drawn through in a loop to the front of the work by means of the hook and when the needle is put downwards through the stuff, laid round it. The needle in its downward and upward passage should be kept in the notch in the thimble and the stuff pressed down with the thimble as the needle is drawn up to the surface of the work, fig. 349.

A little practice is necessary to acquire the right action of the hands, there being always a tendency to confuse the movements of the two. As soon as you realize that the upward drawing of the needle and the downward pressure of the stuff with the thimble must be simultaneous, you will find that you can work with great rapidity and with admirable results. Thread with a very strong twist, which the hook will not split, is the only suitable kind for tambouring. Of the DMC materials, cottons (DMC Brilliant Tatting Cotton or Crochet Cotton) might be preferred.

Numbers of patterns originally intended for other kinds of embroidery can be executed in tambour work; amongst those contained in this Encyclopedia figs. 191, 207, 213, 216, and 224 are the ones that are best adapted to the purpose.

Hooking worked with a crochet needle (Figs. 351, 352, 353). In the chapter on tapestry we remarked that Oriental carpets and mats could be worked in other ways, to be subsequently alluded to at greater length.

Hooking requires only a crochet needle and is worked on coarse canvas linen. Cut your thread into lengths of 8 cm., fold two lengths together in half, stick in the crochet needle from above, under two threads of the canvas, take hold of the loop with the hook, fig. 351, and draw it in; then push out the hook to seize the ends of the cotton and draw them through the loop which is on the needle, as indicated by the arrow in fig. 352. The stitches or tassels should be two or three double threads of the canvas apart. When the whole piece of work is finished shear the entire surface quite even with a pair of sharp scissors. Fig. 353 shows a square of the work completed, presenting that warm velvety appearance which distinguishes many fine carpets.

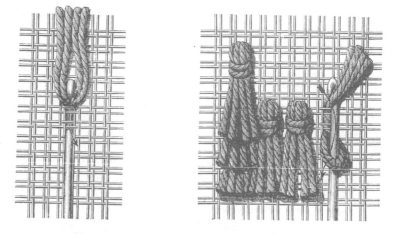

Hooking worked with a crochet needle

Fig. 351. First detail   Fig. 352. Second detail

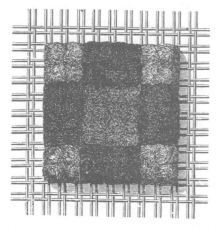

Fig. 353. Appearance of work when finished

Turkey work (figs. 355, 356, 357, 358, 359). It is worked as follows: take a threaded needle under two vertical threads of the stuff from right to left, fig. 355, leaving an end 1 or 2 cm. long, lying on the surface of the work; put the needle in again under the two threads that are in front of the first stitch and leave the tassel formed by the first stitch above the one by which you bring the needle back between the two stitches.

The needle must now follow the same course it took for the first stitch and the thread must be drawn out far enough to form a loop as long as the tassel; you then repeat the second stitch, carrying back the working thread this time above the loop, after which you cut the two open ends the same length as the loop.

154

Fig. 359 represents a portion of a curtain embroidered on Flemish linen in the colours indicated at the foot of the illustration; these may be arranged according to the taste of the worker.

Malta embroidery is mostly done on coarse coloured linen fabrics or on single thread canvas.

In the Maltese work, three times as many threads have to be left between the tassels as are covered by the stitch. Thus if your stitch covers 4 threads of the foundation, you should leave 12 threads between the tassels, and if it covers 6, you should leave an interval of 18 threads, that the stuff may always be visible between the little tassels or balls.

Triangular Turkish or two-sided Turkish stitch (figs. 360, 361, 362, 363, 364). Amongst the many pretty stitches for which Turkish embroideries are distinguished there is one in particular which though apparently very difficult is in reality quite the reverse; in the East it is

Fig. 355. Turkey work. First detail.

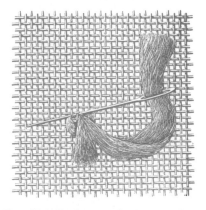

Fig. 356. Turkey work. Second detail.

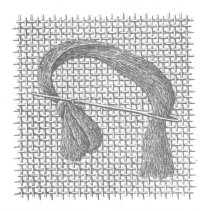

Fig. 357. Turkey work. Third detail.

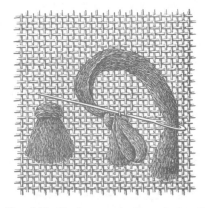

Fig. 358. Turkey work. Fourth detail.

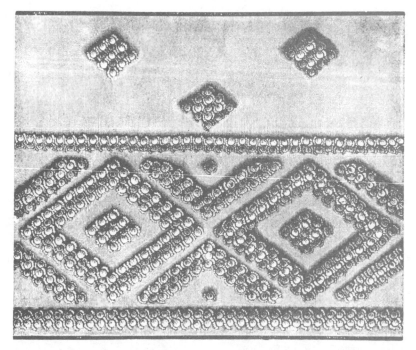

Fig. 359. Malta embroidery. Colours: old gold 725, moss green 469, indigo blue 311 and deep red 902.

generally worked in diagonal lines, each row requiring two journeys to and fro.

In the first, fig. 360, the needle must always be carried first over then under two threads in a diagonal line and so on to the end of the row. Coming back, you pass the needle under the stuff and the stitch on the right side and bring it out at the bottom of the stitch; then you make a back stitch over two horizontal and two vertical threads, pass the needle over two straight threads, put it in behind the same, bring it out again near the upper stitch and then insert it near the bottom vertical stitch; after this you carry it to the second stitch lower down and pass it over the same. Four threads should meet in every hole which the needle makes. The third and fourth row are here worked in a colour that forms a sharp contrast with the one in which the two first rows are worked and constitute with these one complete row of stitches, fig. 361.

Figs. 362, 363, and 364 show how the same stitch can be worked in straight, instead of in diagonal rows.

The dark shade in fig. 364 shows the first and second rows of stitches, the light the third and fourth, as four rows of stitches are required to make one complete row of triangular Turkish stitch.

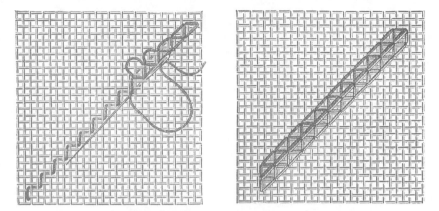

Triangular Turkish stitch worked diagonally

Fig. 360. First journey completed and
second back begun.

Fig. 361. Two journeys to and fro forming
the complete row.

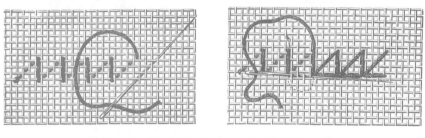

Triangular Turkish stitch worked horizontally

Fig. 362. First journey

Fig. 363. First journey back

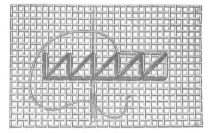

Fig. 364. Second journey back

Pattern worked in triangular Turkish stitch and satin stitch (fig. 365). The diagonal lines are all worked with China golden and blue, and golden and red. The stitch we have just described is most effective in conjunction with other kinds of embroidery, as illustrated in fig. 365, where it is combined with satin stitch.

The running foundation is divided into slanting squares; the diagonal lines are all worked in golden and red. The squares number 9

Fig. 365. Pattern worked in triangular Turkish stitch. Colours: golden 444, indigo blue 311, light blue 775 and green 470.

stitches inside, these are followed by a tenth which is covered by the first stitch of the next square. Where two kinds of golden thread are used, one square will be framed on all sides by one kind, say golden and blue, the next by the other, golden and red.

The stalk that divides the two leaves has a small lozenge at the top and it is begun above the fifth of the 9 stitches; you make 5 stitches in such a manner as to end at the top of these 5 with the stitch that runs in a diagonal direction over the threads, turned to the inside of the stalk, so that the last stitch of the first row may form with the first stitch of the second row a triangle at the top of the stalk, surmounted by the aforesaid lozenge.

The lozenges in golden and light blue, of which there are three in each of the half squares besides those that terminate the stalk, consist of 9 stitches, the first extending over 3 threads, the second over 5, the third over 7, the fourth over 9 and the fifth over 11, the four next decreasing in a similar manner. The leaves in golden and green on either side of the stalk also begin with a stitch over 3 threads of the stuff followed by 8, each increasing in length by one thread on the side of the stalk but all equal on the other, the last extending over 12 threads of the stuff. After these 9, the subsequent 8 must decrease in the same manner by one thread on the opposite side; then you make 4 more extending over only 3 threads and set the contrary way to the others.

The zig-zag border and the small squares of 5 stitches within it are worked entirely in golden and red.

Turkish embroidery (fig. 366). The powdering of flowers and also the border are worked like the preceding pattern in two-sided satin stitch. Embroidery of this kind looks best on linen. It is not absolutely necessary to count the threads for the little flowers and stalks, but it is as well to do so for the border so that you may be sure to get the zig-zags perfectly regular.

The petals of the flowers are worked alternately in golden and red, and golden and blue, the centre and the leaves and stalks in green. The petals are set with stem stitch in black and if the embroidery is to be the same on both sides this setting must be repeated at the back.

The distribution of colours in the border is left to the taste of the worker, but we should recommend for the zig-zags golden and red as being the most effective.

Fig. 366. Turkish embroidery. Colours: golden 444, Cardinal red 606, moss green 470 and black 310.

Appliqué work (fig. 367). Appliqué work means the laying on of pieces of one kind of stuff on to a foundation of a different kind so as to form a pattern – these pieces of stuff of various shapes and sizes taking the place of solid needle-made embroidery.

Appliqué work may be done on linen, silk, velvet, plush and leather. The stuff out of which the pattern is cut has, in some cases, to

Fig. 367. Appliqué work. First part.

be backed first with an iron-on or sew-in interfacing or tissue paper. This is done in the following manner with starch paste, which dries quicker than any other. Spread the paste on the paper with a brush, carefully removing all the little lumps; it should only be just liquid enough to make the stuff and the paper adhere perfectly together and above all must never penetrate to the right side of the stuff. When the paper has been evenly spread with the paste, lay your stuff upon it and smooth and press it down with a clean cloth, stroking it out carefully in the line of the thread to prevent its becoming in the least dragged or puckered and to prevent any air remaining between it and the paper.

You next lay several sheets of paper without a mark or a fold in them on a perfectly smooth flat board, and upon these your paper-lined stuff, covered in its turn with several loose sheets of paper, all being kept in their place by another board with several stones or heavy weights laid upon it to act as a press. Leave the stuff in the press until it be quite dry.

Fig. 367. Appliqué work. Second part.

You will find that any kind of fabric, even the slightest, can be rendered available in this manner for appliqué work, not even plush or velvet being in the least injured by the process.

You then cut out required motifs with a very sharp pair of scissors so as to avoid unravelling the threads along the edges.

Then cover the cut-out figures with paste on the wrong side and fit them into their proper places upon the foundation, stretched in a frame. In larger pieces of work especially, this should be done as quickly as possible so that a board with weights upon it, to serve as a press, may be laid over them all at once.

The board must not be removed until the paste be dry; then you can begin the needlework, fastening down the appliqué figures and finishing them off round the edges by laying down and couching a fine round cord, or by satin stitches.

You either sew on the cord with invisible stitches, opening it a little at each stitch so as to slip the needle and thread in between the twist,

Fig. 368. Morocco embroidery. Colour: Cardinal red 606.

or else with ordinary overcasting stitches. In either case it must be so laid on as completely to hide the cut edges and keep them from fraying.

Should you wish to frame the appliqué figures with flat embroidery, you must bring your needle out close to the cut edge and enter it 1 or 2 mm. within the edge from above.

Both cord and satin stitch setting should be of a subdued shade and, if possible, of a colour to match the foundation.

Morocco embroidery (figs. 368, 369, 370, 371). This work belongs both to the class of darned and damask embroidery.

In fig. 369 the stitches are formed by passing over 5 threads and taking up the sixth. Coming back you take up the third of the 5 threads first missed and proceed in the same manner over the whole surface of the work, unless the lines of the pattern require you to depart from this rule as, for instance, in certain parts of fig. 369, where you will notice stitches carried over 7 or 8 threads; also in the borders, figs. 370 and 371, where the stitches are arranged in a rather arbitrary manner in order to bring out the pattern more clearly.

Fig. 369. Morocco embroidery. Quarter of the subjects of fig. 368.

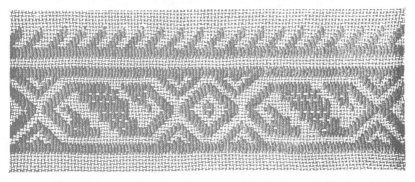

Fig. 370. Morocco embroidery. Small outer border of fig. 368.

Fig. 371. Morocco embroidery. Border and insertion suitable for fig. 368.

163

Fig. 372. Square of Spanish embroidery. Materials and colours: DMC Gold Thread and indigo blue 311, 312 and 334, and pale blue 775.

Fig. 369 represents the fourth part of one of the subjects that make up the design fig. 368; that is, four such, joined together, form one of the squares of fig. 368.

Figs. 370 and 371 are patterns of two borders and an insertion, suitable as a finish to fig. 368, which can be enlarged to any size by the addition of other squares to those that are represented here.

Spanish embroidery (figs. 372 and 373). Some Spanish embroidery consists almost exclusively of button-hole stitch, fig. 170, and flat stitch, fig. 218.   The button-hole stitches, for which the more subdued shade of the colours indicated should always be taken, or else yellow, dark or pale, to match the gold thread, are made over two threads of gold and follow the outlines of the pattern, which should be more or less appropriate to this style of embroidery. One of the gold threads always keeps the inside of the line and follows it throughout in an unbroken course, whilst with the second, the outside one, you form

164

Fig. 373. Quarter of the pattern for fig. 372 in the natural size

picots, folding the gold thread over from right to left and catching down the loop by a button-hole stitch which is introduced into the loop itself and carried over the combined gold threads, as shown in the left corner of fig. 373, representing one quarter of the whole design, where the position of the needle and the way in which the picot is secured are plainly indicated.

Where the picots have to fill up empty spaces of a larger size, you can join several together by connecting them each in turn with the first.

When you have bordered all the outlines with button-hole stitches and picots, fill up the spaces enclosed within the lines, which properly speaking form the pattern, with satin stitch embroidery, worked in Coton à broder or stranded cotton, after which the whole surface is sewn over with fine little spangles which give the sparkling look that constitutes the peculiar charm of this kind of embroidery. The flowers are covered with a fancy stitch that forms small regular lozenges and every second row of stitches is hidden under a spangle.

With regard to the colours indicated at the foot of fig. 372, this is how they were distributed in the original, from which our illustration was taken; all the outlines in button-hole stitch in pale blue; the tops of the flowers in lightest indigo; the bottom parts in medium indigo, and all three shades of blue so blended together in the solid parts of the design as to be undistinguishable from each other. It is not absolutely necessary to keep to the colours here indicated; there is no reason whatever why a greater variety should not be introduced, but in every case the more subdued shades should be selected; a pale red, for instance, for the flowers and a green and a brown for the arabesques will always be found to produce a very pretty and harmonious effect.

When all the needlework is finished, you cut away the stuff underneath the network formed by the picots with a pair of sharp scissors.

A word remains to be said with regard to the copying of fig. 373. Our readers will notice that in fig. 372 the flowers and arabesques succeed and grow out of each other; whilst the four quarters are symmetrical, at the same time curves in each quarter take a different inclination. You cannot therefore simply repeat the subject four times; when you have copied the one quarter, given in fig. 373, you must lay this first quarter on again at the cross + on the left side; when the second quarter is finished, you again turn the copy to the left and tack it on at the +; when you come to the fourth quarter the lines of the first quarter must exactly meet those of the last. We beg here to draw attention to the directions relative to the copying of patterns, given in the subsequent chapter.

Basket stitch on linen (fig. 374). This stitch has some resemblance with the Greek stitch, fig. 273, and the Montenegrin, fig. 301, only that it is not crossed like the latter.

Basket stitch can be worked on all kinds of stuffs, on counted

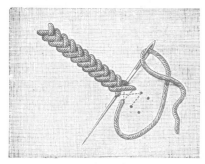
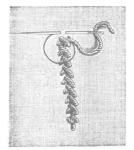

Fig. 374. Basket stitch on linen   Fig. 375. Old German knotted (Coral) stitch

threads or on a wide or narrow tracing, with fine or coarse thread and more or less closely according to the taste of the worker.

You insert the needle in from left to right, and pass it under from 3 to 6 threads of the foundation, according to the stuff and the material you are using, then downwards from left to right, and over from 6 to 8 threads, into the stuff again from right to left; then you push it under the stuff in an upward direction and bring it out on the left in the middle of the space left between the last stitch and the top of the second. The dotted line in the illustration indicates the course of the stitches.

Old German knotted stitch (Coral stitch) (fig. 375). This is a stitch often met with in old church and house linen embroidery. A beautiful design worked in this way is given further on.

Contrary to most stitches, this is worked upwards; the needle is put in horizontally under the stuff, the thread tightly drawn, then laid from left to right and drawn through underneath the first stitch and a tight knot made. We find the same stitch worked in a variety of ways according to the taste and skill of the worker; for instance the knots may be set slanting, as in fig. 375, or else straight and very close together, as in fig. 378, where they present the appearance of a close string of beads, or again wide apart as they are in fig. 381.

All these ways are admissible but care should be taken in each case to make the stitches perfectly regular; it is the direction which is given to the stitch and the number of threads taken up with the needle that changes the appearance of the stitch.

Raised stem stitch (figs. 376, 377). Take a very thick thread and lay it as a foundation thread along the line of your pattern and work over it wide stem stitches, as represented in figs. 171 and 172, either in the same thickness of thread used for the foundation thread, or a finer, according to the stuff you are embroidering upon.

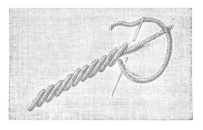

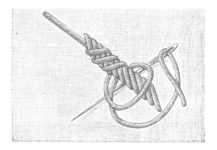

Fig. 377. Another kind
of raised stem stitch

Fig. 376. Raised stem stitch

167

You may overcast the same stitch in the manner indicated in fig. 377, using a different colour for the second layer of stitches to produce an agreeable variety.

Border in different kinds of stitches (fig. 378). The straight lines of this border are all worked in old German knotted stitch in écru thread, forming a thick round cord which stands out from the surface in high relief; the flatter outlining of the outside figures is done in basket stitch in soft blue. The little oblong figures within the two inner lines of the border are worked in satin stitch, in red, and the filling of the figures, outlined in basket stitch, in white button-hole stitch so that all the stitches either enter the stuff or form a network over it.

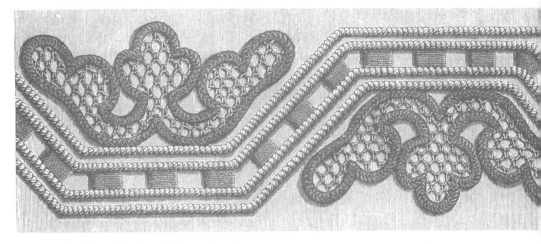

Fig. 378. Border in different kinds of stitches. Colours: 712 écru (Old German knotted stitch), indigo blue 312 (basket stitch), Turkish red 902 (satin stitch) and white (button-hole stitch).

Fig. 379. Roumanian stitch

Roumanian stitch (figs. 379, 380). Though the illustration is so clear as to render it hardly necessary, we subjoin an exact description of the way the stitches run.

Fig. 380. Border in Roumanian stitch. Colours: Cardinal red 606, pomegranate 900, caroub brown 355, Morocco red 321 and 816 or cerise 603 and 600.

Bring out the needle on the left, 2 or 6 threads beyond the line your embroidery is to follow. With regard to the number of threads you take up, you must be guided by the quality of the stuff and the material you have selected: put the needle in on the right, the same distance in advance of the line as before and bring it out in the middle of the stitch; then passing the needle over the first stitch, put it in again one or two threads in advance of the point where it came out, and draw it out close to where the first stitch began.

The border represented in fig. 380 is worked in great part in Roumanian stitch. The original, still very well preserved, notwithstanding its age, is worked in silk of a brilliant red on a stiff stuff which has been coloured by time and use.

Any one of the shades of red named at the foot of the illustration will be found to be a good match for the original colours.

Roumanian stitch is used wherever the lines of the pattern are widest; where they narrow, in the indentures of the leaves and the twists of the stalks, satin stitch is used instead.

By the repetition of the detached subject this pattern may be made to serve either for a stripe or for a grounding; if you use it for a stripe, the centre flower of the principal subject with the stalks lengthened will look very well worked as a separate subject between the large bouquets. Worked in a double row, base to base, on any stuff and in any material, these large figures form a very handsome border which makes an effective trimming for furniture and curtains.

Pattern for piqué embroidery (fig. 381). The stuff called piqué, such as it is now manufactured, is simply an imitation of an old kind of needlework almost unknown in these days but very popular in the fifteenth and sixteenth century in Italy for making coverlets and more especially curtains and blinds, the latter being highly esteemed. A similar kind of work for the making of caps was common in Bohemia

Fig. 381. Pattern for piqué embroidery

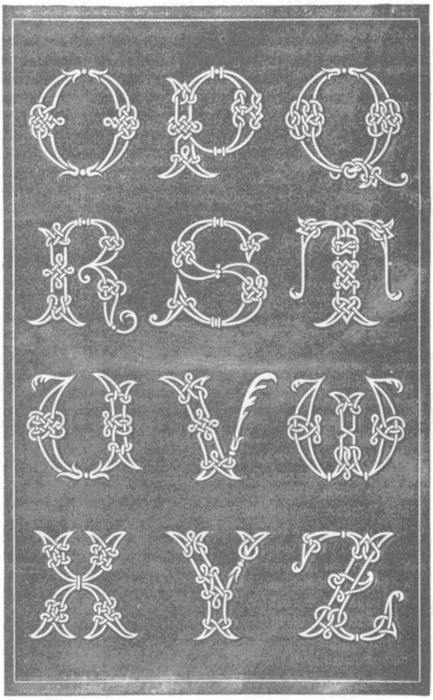

Alphabet in Soutache.

Fig. 382. Letters A to N.   Fig. 383. Letters O to Z.

until a recent date. It is done on two layers of stuff of different kinds, the upper one fine and transparent, the lower more substantial.

The pattern is drawn upon the fine stuff, because on that side the different kinds of stitches are made. You then tack the two stuffs together and work all the outlines of the pattern in Old German knotted stitch with écru sewing thread; that done, thread a crewel needle with white sewing thread or one strand of stranded cotton, slip it in between the two layers of stuff and secure the end by two or three stitches; then push the twist quite close to the knotted stitch and fasten it in between the two layers of stuff, with small and very regular running stitches, in close parallel lines as illustrated, in imitation of piqué stuff.

Fill up in this manner all the ground of the pattern, leaving the arabesques and the ornaments plain, or embellishing them with some kind of lace or embroidery stitch.

When these stripes are intended for blinds, you can produce pretty transparent effects in them by cutting away the underneath stuff in places.

Alphabet in Soutache (braid) (figs. 382, 383, 384, 385, 386, 387). This alphabet, which is one of the best of its kind, was taken from a work published in Venice in 1562 by Giovan' Antonio Tagliente, secretary and calligraphist to the Republic.

171

The letters lend themselves, better than any we know, to being executed in braid or cord.

The sewing on of the braid is done with very small running stitches and the interlacing with a tapestry needle, into which the braid is threaded; both operations are shown in figs. 384 and 385. The embroidery of the connecting bars and the small leaves and tendrils that complete the letter are explained in fig. 386, whilst fig. 387 represents the letter A in its finished state.

Flowers executed in Soutache and embroidery (fig. 388). Flowers and sprays, such as here represented, make a charming trimming for summer dresses, sunshades, aprons, etc. and can be executed with admirable effect in braid or cord. A very pretty running pattern can be formed out of the spray, fig. 388, by turning the flowers first to the right and then to the left and making the stalks come out underneath the ears of corn. In order to reverse the position of the flowers thus you will have to make two tracings of the spray, one negative and one positive.

For the ears of corn in fig. 388, use either écru, or ochre-coloured braid; for the marguerites, white Soutache and for the cornflowers, indigo blue braid. Nothing could be simpler than the mode of working these flowers.

Thread a tapestry needle with the braid and draw it into the stuff, and then pass it through from the right side to the wrong at the bottom of one of the petals of the flowers, secure it on the wrong side by two or three stitches and then bring the working thread, which should be of the same colour as the braid, out again at the point of the petal, then carry the braid back to the bottom of the petal and fasten it down, as in fig. 239, by a stitch rather wider than the braid, fold the braid over again to the starting point, and secure it by a stitch, and so on. In order to give a different character to the flowers, use braid of different widths, fold it over more or less closely and lay it down in shorter or longer lengths as required. The natural irregularity of the petals of a flower can be very faithfully imitated in this manner. Fig. 388 shows the way in which, for the ears of corn, the braid is folded back upon itself and fastened down, whilst in the white flowers the two layers of the braid that form each petal are separated at the bottom.

The stamens of the marguerites are worked in knot stitch with yellow cotton and those of the cornflowers with dark blue. The other little details are executed in satin and stem stitch in the colours indicated at the foot of the illustration. With the pattern to go by, the distribution of the colours for the different parts can present no possible difficulty.

Fig. 384. Letter T of the Soutache alphabet. Mode of interlacing the Soutache.

Fig. 385. Letter M of the alphabet in Soutache. Mode of sewing on the braid.

Fig. 386. Letter W Mode of placing the bars and embroidering the leaves.

Fig. 387. Letter A of the alphabet in its finished state

We need only point out that the Cardinal red is intended for the little knot that connects the stalks of the flowers.

Fig. 388. Flowers executed in Soutache and embroidery. Colours: braids for Soutache work in white, écru, ochre and indigo blue, and embroidery threads (preferably Coton à Broder) écru 712, orange-yellow 972, indigo blue 311, lime green 704 and 699, pistachio 966, 702 and 699 and Cardinal red 606.

173

Chinese subject (fig. 389). This quaint and graceful composition, copied from an interesting piece of Chinese embroidery, gives our readers the opportunity of turning the different damask stitches, already described in these pages, to quite a new use. It can be worked on gauze or fine evenweave linen, the threads of which can be counted.

The drawing has to be transferred to the stuff, and the different parts are filled in with the stitches, clearly indicated in the illustration.

By the introduction of several colours, this pattern is capable of being infinitely varied. Thus, in the model before us, the neck and bulb of the flask, the leaves it stands upon and those attached to the flowers in it, are worked in pistachio 966; the handles, the ornament on the bottle and the triangular figure in the centre are in white; the little flower on the left, the second on the right, the straight staff, the upper wings of the butterfly as well as the three leaves underneath the triangle are in indigo blue 334; the first flower on the right of the flask, the knot above the triangle, the lower wings of the butterfly and the middle part of the bottom subject on the right of the illustration are in mid-grey 318; Lees red 315 and caroub brown 355 alternate in the pointed leaves that support the flask; the former colour recurs in the ornaments of the staff, and Cardinal red 606, black 310 and Lime 704 alternate in the other details of the drawing.

For the setting it will be best to take DMC Gold Embroidery Thread, used either double or single, according to whichever the drawing seems to require.

Fig. 389. Chinese subject

174

Ornament after Holbein

Practical Directions

Hitherto we have been chiefly occupied with descriptions and explanations of the different kinds of needlework; to render these complete, it remains for us to give a few practical directions with regard to the copying, adjustment and transposition of the patterns, as well as to the different processes often so essential to the ultimate success of a piece of needlework.

Tracing patterns against a window pane. In order to copy a pattern in this way, the first step is to tack or pin the piece of stuff or paper on which the copy is to be made upon the pattern. In the case of a small pattern, the tacking or pinning may be dispensed with and the two sheets held firmly pressed against the window pane with the left hand, whilst the right hand does the tracing, but even then it is safer to pin the four corners of the two sheets together as, in case of interruption, it is difficult to fit them together again exactly.

The tracing may be done with a pencil, or better still, an artist's pen or water-colour paint.

The process of tracing is easy enough so long as the hand does not get tired but as this generally comes to pass very soon it is best, if the pattern be a large and complicated one, temporarily to stick the sheets to the pane.

To take off a pattern by tracing. If you want to take a pattern of a piece of embroidery direct from the work itself, lay it, the right side up, flat upon a board or table and cover it with tracing paper. Carefully, so as not to apply too much pressure on the needlework beneath, trace the design with a soft pencil or artist's pen.

To transfer a pattern direct on to the stuff. Patterns cannot be copied by either of the above methods direct on to the stuff unless the

175

embroidery to be executed is transparent; in the case of thick close fabrics the prick-and-pounce method, described below, may be used.

To pounce patterns upon stuffs. The patterns, after having been transferred to strong paper, have to be pricked through. To do this you lay the paper upon cloth or felt and prick out all the lines of the drawing with a needle, making the holes, which should be clear and round, all exactly the same distance apart.

The closer and more complicated the pattern is, the finer and closer the holes should be. Every line of the outline must be carefully pricked out. A symmetrical design can be folded together into four and all pricked at once.

The pricked pattern has next to be tacked upon the material, the side from which the pricking was done next to the stuff and the little funnel-shaped holes uppermost. Paper and stuff must be firmly fastened down and kept in position so that neither of them may move during the process, otherwise you will have double lines on the stuff which you will find very confusing afterwards.

For the pouncing, use either powdered chalk or charcoal, according to whether the stuff be dark or light in colour. Dip the pouncing implement, a thing like a small drum-stick, stuffed and covered with cloth, into the powder and rub it lightly over the whole surface of the pricked pattern, so that the powder penetrates through the pin-holes to the stuff. In default of a proper pouncing implement take a small strip of cloth, roll it up round a stick and wind a string round, and dip this into the powder.

When the powder has penetrated to the stuff, remove the paper and if the pattern is to be repeated, lay it on again further on, taking care to make the lines meet exactly so that the join may not be seen.

When you have finished the pouncing and taken off the paper, you proceed to draw or rather paint in the pattern with water-colour paints. Four paints, blue, black, yellow and white are sufficient for all purposes, whatever the colour of the stuff may be.

On a smooth surface the tracing may be done with a pen but a small sable-hair brush is preferable under all circumstances. The rougher and more hairy the surface, the finer the brush ought to be, in order that the colour may sink well in between the fibres. Before beginning to paint in the pattern, gently blow away all the superfluous powder from the surface.

The preparation of the stuffs and the subdivision of the patterns. Long years of experience and practice have brought us in contact with a good many designers, many of them artists so long as it was only a question of putting their own compositions on paper but who yet found themselves confronted by real difficulties the moment they were called upon to transfer them to stuff.

We shall, as far as possible, point out to our readers the precautions to be taken in tracing patterns and must for that purpose go back to one of the first operations, namely that of pricking.

To begin with, the paper on which the pattern is should always be large enough for there to be a clear margin of from 4 to 5 cm. all round the pattern, so that the pouncing instrument may never come in contact with the stuff beneath.

In transferring patterns to stuff, no lines of division should ever be made directly upon it either with lead, chalk or charcoal, as it is hardly ever possible entirely to obliterate them and they often become very confusing afterwards.

Before beginning the tracing, divide your stuff into four, then decide what the width of the border outside the pattern is to be; it is quite an exceptional thing to carry a pattern right up to the edge. Stuffs that will take a bend, such as all linen and cotton textures, can be folded in four, like the paper, the folds ought then to be pinched and pressed down so that the lines may remain clear and distinct until the tracing be finished. After dividing it into four, mark out the diagonal lines; these are absolutely necessary in order to get the corner figures rightly placed.

Though most of our readers know how to make these lines on paper with a pencil and ruler, few, easy as it is, know how to make them upon stuff. You have only to fold over the corner of your piece of stuff so that the outside thread of the warp or cut edge runs parallel with the woof edge which marks the angle of the fold-over.

This double folding over divides the ground into 8 parts. To arrange for the outside border or margin is easy enough if the stuff and the kind of work you are going to do upon it admit of the drawing out of threads, as then a thread drawn out each way serves as a guide for tracing the pattern, straight to the line of the stuff. It is often better, however, not to draw out the threads for an open-work border till the pattern be traced. If you do not wish or are not able to draw out threads to mark the pattern and you are working on a stuff of which the threads can be counted, follow the directions given below.

You cannot mark cloth, silk stuffs or plush by folding them in the above way, cloth and some kinds of silken textures will not take a bend and others that will would be spoiled by it. All such stuffs should be mounted in a frame before the pattern be traced and the ground be then divided out in the following way: take a strong thread, make a knot at one end, stick a pin into it and tighten the knot round it; with a pair of compasses, divide one of the sides into two equal parts, stick the pin with the knot round it in at the middle and the same on the opposite side, putting in a second pin by means of which you stretch the thread; carry other threads across in a similar way, in the width of the stuff and from corner to corner and you will have your ground correctly marked out in such a manner as to leave no marks when, after pouncing in the pattern, you remove the threads. Before finishing the pouncing of a pattern see that it is the right size for the purpose it is intended for.

Supposing that you are tracing a border with a corner, you should measure the length it will occupy, and then by a very light pouncing you can mark the points from which the pattern will have to be repeated. It may be that a gap will be left in the middle which, if not too large, can be got rid of without altering the pattern by pushing the whole thing a little further in and so shortening the distance between the two corners.

Should the gap, however, be too large for this you will have to make a supplementary design to fill up the place. The same thing would be necessary in the case of your having to shorten a pattern.

To transpose and repeat patterns by means of looking-glasses (fig. 390). We have referred to the necessity that often occurs of adapting patterns to certain given proportions; this can in most cases be done easily enough without the help of a draughtsman, especially in the case of cross-stitch embroideries, by means of two unframed looking-glasses (Penelope mirrors, as they are called) used in the following manner.

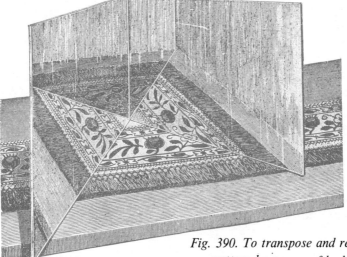

Fig. 390. To transpose and repeat a straight pattern by means of looking glasses

178

If you want to utilize only a piece of a straight border or, after repeating it several times, to form a corner with it, you place the mirror in the first instance across it at right angles, at the place from which the pattern is to be repeated, and then exactly diagonally inwards.

To make a square out of a straight pattern, you take two mirrors and so place them that they touch at the point where the diagonal lines meet, as represented in fig. 390, and you have your square at once.

This is all easy enough, but before beginning any large piece of work it is necessary to consider carefully which parts of the drawing will best fill the centre and which are best suited to form the corners, as it is not every part of a straight pattern that is adapted for repetition.

A few preliminary trials with the help of the mirrors will better show the importance of these explanations than anything further we can say on the subject.

Similarly, the placing of one unframed looking-glass gives you a corner design.

To alter the proportions of a pattern by dividing the ground into squares (figs. 391 and 392). Cases will occur where it will be found necessary to subject the pattern to greater modifications still than those we have hitherto been dealing with.

You want, for example, to embroider a rather large running ground pattern on a piece of stuff that is relatively too small for the subject, or a small and rather minute pattern on a large surface on which it is likely to look either too insignificant or too crowded and confused, and the chances are, if you do not know how to draw, you will either think it necessary to get a draughtsman to help you or you will give up the piece of work altogether, deterred by the difficulties that confront you. You need not do either if you will follow the directions here given.

Take a sheet of large-sized graph paper which if necessary you can prepare for yourself and trace your pattern upon it, or rule squares direct upon the drawing, as shown in fig. 391.

Then take a second sheet of graph paper with squares a fourth, a third or half as small again as those on the first sheet. Thus, if the sides of the first squares be 15 mm. long and you want to reduce your pattern by one fifth, the sides of your new squares should measure only 12 mm.

If, on the contrary, you want to enlarge the pattern by one fifth, make the sides of your squares 18 mm. long.

Then you follow, square by square, the lines of the drawing,

Fig. 391. Dividing the ground into squares before copying

extending or contracting them according to whether the pattern is to be enlarged or diminished.

To copy a pattern directly from a piece of embroidery and enlarge or diminish it at the same time, proceed as follows: fix the embroidery on a board, stretching it equally in every direction; then measure the length of the drawing, divide the centimetres by the number of units corresponding to whatever the proportions of your copy are to be, and if there be any fractions of centimetres over, subdivide them into millimetres and, if necessary, into half millimetres and make your division by whatever measure you have adopted; take a pair of compasses with dry points, open them sufficiently for the opening to correspond to the number and the distance obtained by the division; plant a pin with a thread fastened to it at the point indicated by the point of the compasses and repeat the last operation all along one side of the embroidery and if possible a little beyond it so that it may not be defaced by the marks of the pins. All you now have to do is to pull the threads in perfectly straight lines to the opposite side and carry other threads across them in a similar manner so that the whole surface be divided into squares.

It is needless to say that if you have to trace a pattern from a mounted piece of work you cannot stretch it on a board; with a little

Fig. 392. Pattern reduced by marking out the ground in small squares

invention, however, some way can always be found of planting the pins so as not to injure the work.

To alter the width of a pattern retaining the original height (figs. 393, 394, 395). Sometimes it is necessary to lengthen a pattern without, however, altering its height. In this case you modify the shape of the square and make long or narrow squares according to the general shape of the design you wish to reproduce. Fig. 393 represents a pattern in Soutache marked out in squares; in fig. 394 the squares are lengthened out a third beyond their original size and the pattern is

Fig. 393. Pattern in Soutache. Original size.

Fig. 394. Pattern in fig. 393 drawn out in the width

Fig. 395. Pattern in fig. 393 compressed in the width

181

expanded; in fig. 395, the squares are compressed to a third less than their original size.

To prepare the paste for appliqué work. It may seem strange to devote a separate section to such an apparently simple operation; but in appliqué work it is a most important one, as not only the stuff on which the work is done but all the expensive accessories are liable to be spoilt by paste that has been badly prepared.

Put some wheaten (not rice) starch into a vessel with a rounded bottom, pour on just enough water to dissolve the starch and stir it with a wooden spoon till it becomes perfectly smooth.

In the meantime put about a quarter of a pint of clean water to boil and when it boils add to it a little powdered pitch or carpenter's glue, in quantity about the size of a pea, and pour in the starch, stirring it the whole time. When the mixture has boiled up several times take it off the fire and go on stirring it till it gets cold otherwise lumps will form in it which, as we specially pointed out, must never be allowed to get in between the stuff and the paper.

This kind of paste makes no spots and does not injure even the most delicate colours as it contains no acid. In winter it will keep for several days but in hot weather it very soon begins to ferment and should then on no account be used.

When the work is finished it is a good plan to spread a very thin layer of paste over the entire back of it with a fine brush made of hogs' bristles, and not to take it out of the frame until it is perfectly dry.

To wash coloured cottons and work done with the same. In order to test the fastness of the dyes, untie the skeins and pour boiling water upon them, leave them to soak for about a quarter of an hour, soap and rub them lightly with the hand from end to end and rinse them out thoroughly in as many changes of cold water as may be found necessary until the water remain perfectly colourless.

Squeeze out all the water you can and let them dry quickly without exposing them to the sun.

Coloured cottons are often washed in vinegar because it is supposed to affect the colour less than water does. We have come to the conclusion after several trials that this is a delusion, for the good dyes keep their colour without the aid of vinegar and the bad ones wash out in spite of it.

If a piece of work has been done with unwashed cottons and the colours run in the first washing, you have only to rinse it out in several changes of tepid water to restore it to its original freshness, and if you want a yellowish tinge it should be dipped in weak tea or coffee.

Double chevron smocking stitch

Further Stitches
& Useful Information

Beginning a new thread with the waste knot method (fig. 396). This method is increasingly used in canvaswork and in any fairly dense embroidery on fabric, such as solid cross-stitching. As the illustrations show, the knotted thread is taken in from the right side of the fabric ideally along the line along which you are next going to stitch. The first few stitches you take are therefore worked over that thread, on the back of your fabric. When you reach the knot, slightly pull the knot and snip it off.

If you are stitching on canvas it is advisable, certainly, to take the waste knot in exactly vertically or horizontally, that is to say parallel with warp or weft threads.

Ending a thread with the waste tail method (fig. 397). A thread can similarly be finished with a 'wasted tail'. When you have only a few

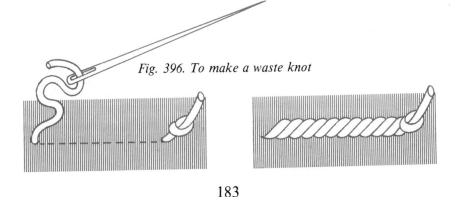

Fig. 396. To make a waste knot

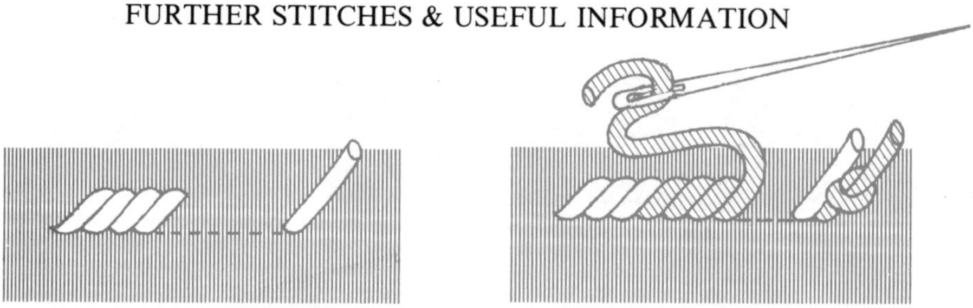

Fig. 397. Similarly, a thread can be finished with a waste tail. The waste knot of the next thread (here shaded) can be taken in from the same place.

inches of thread left, bring it up to the right side of the fabric, ideally along the line along which you are next going to stitch and, if you are working on canvas, certainly parallel with warp or weft threads. You do not need to knot this thread tail: you can hold it with your free hand.

Start your next thread with a waste knot, taken in at the same point from which the waste tail emerged. Your first few stitches of this next thread will accommodate both tail and knot lengths on the back of the work and when you reach the suitable point cut off both tail end and knot.

Raised or stumpwork. Especially in the last three-quarters of the seventeenth century in England, gentlewomen formed three-dimensional motifs, sometimes barely an inch across, which were applied to white satin panels.

Sometimes wooden or wire shapes were embellished with open button-hole and other embroidery techniques. In other instances stitching was worked directly on to the stuff.

Cup stitch (fig. 398) was among the many stitches found on raised work at this time.

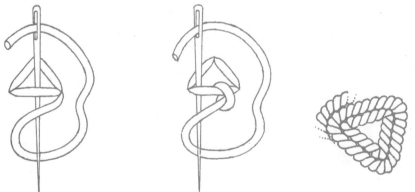

Fig. 398. Forms made in cup stitch rise above the stuff on which they are being worked

Fig. 399. The outer ring of a two-ringed hoop is placed above the stuff, the inner ring beneath it. The fabric is gently pulled taut before the screw is finally tightened.

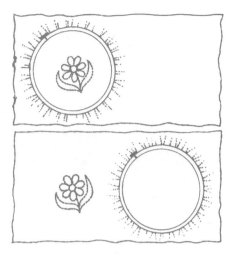

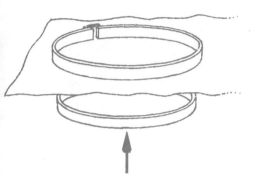

Fig. 400. One of the many advantages of a ring hoop is that it can be moved from one part of the stuff to another

Modern frames and hoops (figs. 399, 400). Many people today like to work with stuff on a lightweight and easily portable ring hoop, the best of which consist of two rings of moulded plastic, the outer of which has a slight ridge on the inside and the inner a slight ridge on the outside so that the stuff is held taut between the hoops when clipped together.

The inner ring is placed beneath the stuff and the outer ring above the stuff as shown (fig. 399). If the stuff is carefully pulled taut before the screw is finally tightened the stuff will less likely be 'marked'.

One advantage of an easily portable ring hoop is that it can be removed from one part of the stuff to another.

Canvas should never be placed in a circular hoop. It must always be held with a square or oval frame.

As well as the laced frames already referred to, there is now a wide selection of roller frames and bars, and some people simply staple-gun or T-pin canvas to a frame formed from two pairs of artists' stretchers.

More canvaswork information (fig. 401). Some people today like to work on interlock or lockthread canvas. This has two fine warp threads locked around a single weft thread. Because it does not, therefore, distort during stitching interlock canvas can be hand-held rather than put in a frame.

It has already been stated that tent stitch is probably the most

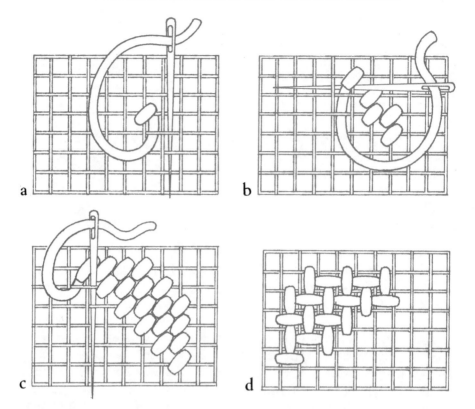

a

b

c

d

Fig. 401. Basketweave tent stitch: the last illustration shows the reverse of the work.

popular canvaswork technique and this is specially so in North America. Here, as elsewhere, many people work it in diagonal rows which produces a 'basketweave' formation on the reverse. This method of working tent stitch causes less distortion than stitching in horizontal rows (continental method).

Scandinavian embroidery. Among the many types of needlework associated with Scandinavia are Hardanger and Hedebo.

Hardanger is recognisable for a trellised ground bordered by overcastings of blocks of satin stitch, say five stitches each over four pairs of threads or nine stitches each over eight threads of the stuff. Extra decoration within a hardanger motif can be provided by lace star filling stitch (as in fig. 402) or a spider's web.

Hedebo, another cutwork, has circular areas cut radially as shown, the segments then turned back and held with a form of button-hole stitch (fig. 403). Interior bars can then be formed from one part of the circumference to another: a thread is taken to and fro several times and bound with the same hedebo button-hole stitch.

186

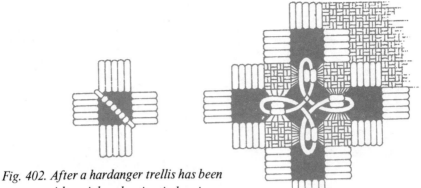

Fig. 402. After a hardanger trellis has been overcast with peripheral satin stitches, it can be partly infilled with a lace star filling.

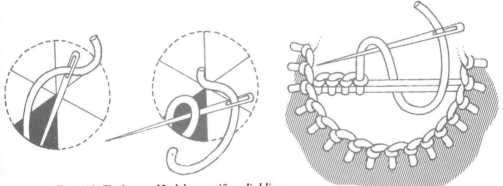

Fig. 403. To form a Hedebo motif, radial lines are cut in a marked circle: each segment is turned back and bound with Hedebo button-hole stitch.

Florentine work (fig. 404). Also known as Bargello and sometimes Irish stitch, this consists of parallel rows of differently coloured vertical satin stitches. It is generally worked on canvas.

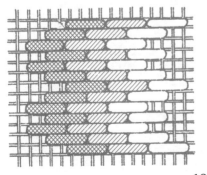

Fig. 404. Florentine is characterised by differently coloured parallel rows of satin stitches

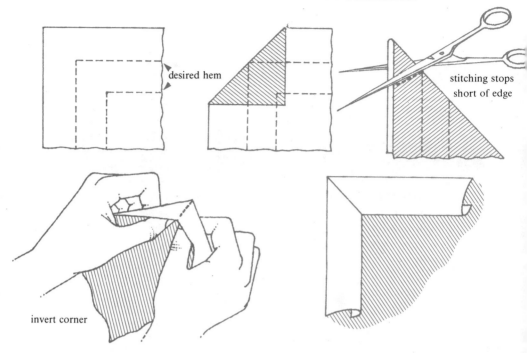

Fig. 405. How to mitre a corner of stuff (wrong side of stuff here shaded)

Counted thread. This name refers to any needlework on stuff of which threads are counted, e.g. cross-stitch embroidery. Some whiteworks are counted, so too are many blackworks, usually characterised as black-on-white needleworks.

How to mitre the corners of fabric (fig. 405). One indispensable needlework skill, unfortunately rare now that linen tablecloths are a thing of the past, is that of mitre-ing corners of a cloth. The illustrations here speak for themselves.

Smocking (fig. 406). Gathers (q.v.) can be embellished with decorative stitching, generally variations of stem stitch with horizontal rows formed of stitches worked over one or two gathers in an arranged pattern.

Quilting (fig. 407). What appears to be running stitches worked in 'stab' style, with separate movements of the needle in and out of the stuff, holds two or more layers of stuff together, sometimes with padding between. Forms of quilting include Italian, with two parallel lines of stitching through two layers of stuff and with cord subsequently threaded, from the back of the work, through the

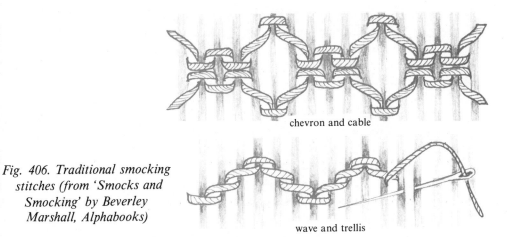

chevron and cable

Fig. 406. Traditional smocking stitches (from 'Smocks and Smocking' by Beverley Marshall, Alphabooks)

wave and trellis

channels thus formed, and trapunto, in which areas of a design are similarly padded, after stitching, from behind.

Materials. We conclude our work with the well-meant and by no means useless recommendation to our readers never to begin a piece of work of any considerable size without first making sure that the colours they intend to use are fast and providing themselves with a larger supply of materials than even on a close calculation they think they are likely to require, lest they should find themselves under the disagreeable necessity of having either to leave their work unfinished or finish it with materials that do not match. There is generally a slight difference in tone between cottons that have been bought at different times, and it is therefore important to make sure you buy ample material before you start a project.

DMC as such does not manufacture either canvas or evenweave or other fabrics. If you do not have a suitable local shop you might like to contact either of these establishments, both of which offer mail order facilities: Mace & Nairn, 89 Crane Street, Salisbury, Wiltshire SP1

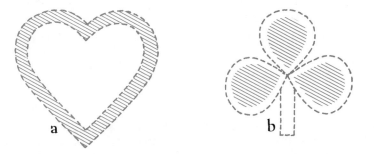

a   b

Fig 407. Italian quilting A, and trapunto B. The padded areas are shaded.

189

2PY; or The Silver Thimble, 33 Gay Street, Bath, Avon BA1 2NT. In America, The World in Stitches, 82 South Street, Milford, NH 03055, USA, has an especially detailed catalogue.

Threads. To many people 'DMC' is now synonymous with six-stranded stranded cotton, known in America as 'floss'. This comes in 8 metre skeins bound by two paper bands, one of which has an illustration of which end of the long thread to pull.

Stranded cotton has no 'nap' and you can stitch from either end of a pulled length, say about 38 cm. You can stitch with one, two, three, four, five or all of the six strands. Since the entire thickness is quite tightly twisted, however, it is a good idea – regardless of how many strands you will stitch – first to 'strip' the thread. To strip your thread, first cut off a required length and then carefully pull out, from one end, one and then another and another strand until all six strands are separated. You then lay back together as many strands as required. 'Stripped' stranded cotton produces much smoother stitches which better 'cover' the stuff.

Other DMC threads suitable for embroideries are:

DMC Brilliant Pearl Cotton sizes 3 (skeins 15 metres) and 5 (skeins 25 metres), or sizes 5, 8, 12 (balls of 10 g., ⅜ oz).

DMC Brilliant Embroidery Cotton (Coton à Broder) and cutwork thread. Sizes 12 and 16 (skeins 23 metres), and 20 and 25 (skeins 32 metres).

DMC Soft Embroidery Twist, size 4 (skeins 10 metres).

DMC Tapestry wool (skeins 8 metres).

DMC Tapestry grounding wool (5 hanks of 20g.).

DMC Gold Embroidery Thread and DMC Silver Embroidery Thread are both available in reels of 5g. (³⁄₁₆ oz). DMC Divisible Gold or Silver Embroidery Thread is available in spools of 40 metres. They are lastingly brilliant (they do not tarnish), heatproof up to at least 180° C (356° F) and they are washable in lukewarm warm water; they can be ironed and dry-cleaned.

Full details of the current range of DMC materials can be obtained from one of the above-mentioned shops. Retailers and those interested in stocking DMC products should contact one of the following: Dunlicraft Ltd., Pullman Road, Wigston, Leicester, LE8 2DY; DMC, 107 Trumbull Street, Elizabeth, NJ 07206, USA; DMC, Mulhouse, Haut Rhin R, France.

Index

INDEX

renaissance – *contd*
fifteenth century 1.14.1; 7.4.3; 10.2.2; 11.2.2
twelfth century 1.14; 8.6.13; 9.2.1
répertoires 16.5.3–4
repetitiones 4.3.1; 4.4.4
Repgow, Eike von. *See* Eike
reports of cases 8.7.5; 11.3.6–9; 12.4.2–5; 14.2.10; 14.3.5–6; 16.5.2–3
Representation of the People Acts 1918 & 1928 18.3.3. *See also* Reform Acts
reprisal, right of 6.5.2; 6.5.7
Requests, Court of 8.9.10
Révigny, Jacques de. *See* Jacques
Revolution. *See* French; Industrial
Rhineland 15.7.11; 16.4.1; 16.5.4
Ribuarian/Ripuarian Franks and their law 1.5.3
Roffredus Beneventanus (of Benevento) (d.1242) 3.5.6; 3.7.15; 3.8.4; 5.5.4; 7.2.2; App 1(c)
Roger (Rogerius) (d.1192) 3.8.3; 7.5.1
Rolandino Passagieri (d.1300) 5.5.4; 7.2.2
Rôles d'Oléron 6.3.5
Roman-Dutch law 13.4.3; 13.4.4–5; 13.4.7. *See also* Dutch law
Roman Empire 1A; 2.1.2; 2.5.1; 5.1.3; 8.2.1; 11.2.2; 13.3.5; 18.5.1
jurists 1.1; 1.2.2; 3.3.4; 16.2.7
law, classical 1.1; 1.2.2; 1.3.1; 3.2.1; 10.2.7; 10.5.5; 11.4.3; 16.2.3; 16.2.7; 16.2.9–10; 16.3.6; 16.5.6
general influence 1.3.1–2; 1.8.3–4; 1.11.3–7; 1.12.3; 1.14; 2.1.3; 2.9; 3 *passim*; 4 *passim*; 5.1.3; 5.2.3; 5.5.3; 5.6.4; 5.8.1; 5.8.5; 5.9.2; 5.9.4; 6.2; 6.3.6; 6.6.8–9; 7.2.1; 7.5.2–3; 7.6.2; 7.6.5; 8.1.2; 9.6.4; 10.2.7; 10.5.8; 10.8.4–5; 11.2; 11.3.3; 11.4.3–4; 11.5.5–6; 12.1.1; 12.1.4; 12.2.2; 12.2.5; 13.2.10; 13.3.6; 13.4.2–7; 13.5.3; 14.1.4; 14.1.10; 15.2.1; 15.2.3; 15.2.6; 15.4.4–5; 15.6.1; 15.6.3–4; 15.7.1–3; 15.7.7; 16.2.3–4; 16.3.1; 16.4.5; 16.4.8
Justinianic 1.2.2; 1.14.4; 3.2.1; 10.2.7; 10.5.5; 16.2.7
survival through the Dark Ages 1.11; 2.1.3
vulgar 1.3; 1.5.2; 7.3.8
see also reception of Roman law
Republic 1.1.1
Romania 7.1.2; 15.6.5

romano-canonical procedure. *See* procedure, romano-canonical
Rome 1.2.1; 1.3.4; 1.4.3; 1.6.3; 1.7.1; 1.9.2; 1.11.1; 1.14.4; 3.8.4; 5.4.4; 6.4.1; 6.4.3; 7.3.7; 10.1.3; 16.1.3–4. *See also* Papacy
Roncaglia, Diet of (1158) 2.4.6; 3.7.13
Rota, Court of the Sacred Roman 5.7.2; 7.3.7
Rothari of the Lombards (636–52) and his *Edict* 1.8.2; 1.14.2
Rouen 7.5.7
Rousseau, Jean-Jacques (1712–78) 15.2.4
Roxburgh 9.4.4
royal jurisdiction 2.5.1–2; 2.8.2–4. *See also* kingship
Rufinus (d.1192) 5.3.6; 5.6.1
Russia 7.1.2; 10.1.2; 15.2.6; 16.6.4; 18.4.2–3; 18.5.2

Sachsenspiegel 2.9.5; 7.4.3; 11.1.6–8; 11.1.10; 11.2.3; 15.4.1
Sächsische Weichbild 11.1.10
St Andrews 2.7.4; 7.7.1; 14.1.8; 14.1.12
St Gall, *Epitome* of 1.5.3
St German, Christopher (c.1460–1540) 13.5.1
St Ives, fair court of 6.4.6; 6.5.6; 6.5.7; 6.5.8
sake and soke 8.3.3; 9.4.2
Salamanca 7.6.2; 7.6.3; 13.2.3
Salatiele (and the *Ars notariatus*) (fl.1236–74) 3.7.2; 7.2.2
Sale of Goods Act 1893 (c.71) 16.4.9
Salerno 1.14.6; 3.8.4; 6.3.1
Salic law 1.5.3; 1.9.4
Salzburg 7.1.2
sanctuary 10.8.6
Saracens 6.3.1. *See also* Arabs; Moslems
Sardinia 1.7.1; 1.10.3; 6.3.1; 16.1.4. *See also* Piedmont
sasine 2.3.1. *See also* feudal institutions
instrument of 14.5.6
Savigny, Friedrich Carl von (1779–1861) 3.5.1; 17.1.2; 16.2.3–8; 16.2.11; 16.3.3; 16.3.5; 16.5.4
Savoy 13.4.7
Saxony and Saxons 1.9.3; 1.10.1; 1.10.5; 1.12.1; 1.13.3; 2.9.5; 7.4.1; 7.4.3; 8.1.2; 8.2.1; 10.1.4; 11.1.6–8; 11.1.10; 11.1.12; 11.2.3; 11.3.5; 11.3.6; 11.4.3; 11.4.4; 11.5.2; 11.5.5; 15.4.1; 16.4.1. *See also Sachsenspiegel*
scabini (doomsmen) 2.6. *See also échevins*; *Schöffen*